WITHDRAWN

VISION
of the voyage

VISION of the voyage

Hart Crane and the Psychology of Romanticism

by Robert Combs

MEMPHIS STATE UNIVERSITY PRESS

Hart Crane quotations are taken from *The Complete Poems and Selected Letters and Prose of Hart Crane,* edited by Brom Weber, with ther permission of Liveright Publishing Corporation. Copyright 1933, © 1958, 1966 by Liveright Publishing Corporation.

Library of Congress Cataloging in Publication Data

Combs, Robert Long, 1945-
  Vision of the voyage.

  Includes bibliographical references and index.
  1. Crane, Hart, 1899-1932—Criticism and interpretation. 2. Romanticism. 1. Title.
  PS3505.R272Z64   811'.5'2   77-25535
  ISBN 0-87870-034-X

Copyright © 1978 by Memphis State University Press

All rights reserved. No part of this book may be reproduced or utilized in any form or by any means, electronic or mechanical, including photocopying and recording, or by any information storage and retrieval system without permission from the publisher.

Manufactured in the United States of America

In thus concentrating itself on itself, Spirit is engulfed in the night of its own self-consciousness; its vanished existence is, however, conserved therein; and this superseded existence—the previous state, but born anew from the womb of knowledge—is the new stage of existence, a new world, and a new embodiment or mode of Spirit. Here it has to begin all over again at its immediacy, as freshly as before, and thence rise once more to the measure of its stature, as if, for it, all that preceded were lost, and as if it had learned nothing from the experience of the spirits that preceded.

Hegel
The Phenomenology of Mind

To
My Mother and Father

Contents

Preface *page* ix
1. Main Currents in Romantic Psychology 1
2. *White Buildings:* The Character of Crane's Lyric 33
3. *The Bridge:* The Meaning of Suffering 109
   Epilogue: Against Conclusions 175
   Index *page* 179

Preface

When Hart Crane died in 1932 he left his reading public an enigma which is perhaps indecipherable. Since then writers and critics have tried to reconstruct the "fabulous shadow" of Crane's life. But they have been divided between an admiration for his occasional lyric brilliance on the one hand, and a mistrust of the deeper implications in his whole poetic vision on the other. Crane's poetry has been acclaimed and denounced with equal passion. To Tennessee Williams, for example, he has served as a kind of twentieth-century saint. To others, like Allen Tate, he has been a negative example—what a poet of certain leanings may unfortunately become. In response to the latter opinion, a number of critical books have been written attempting to vindicate the impulse of Crane's idealism, even if it produced an imperfect poetry. But these books continue to rely, at least in part, on Crane's own arguments about the worth of his endeavor, which he wrote to Otto Kahn and other influential people. And, more importantly, these efforts to champion Crane have propagated a myth that is difficult to take seriously except in an exalted frame of mind. This is the role of the poet as heroic redeemer. The assumptions behind the concept are, of course, religious. The poet is seen as a kind of priest who, while he opposes the

Preface

Philistines, offers to the believer through the poem a higher, deeper, or truer experience of life than the believer could achieve for himself without the poet-priest's assistance. Common to both poet and priest is a belief in some special Truth, a Word waiting to be embodied symbolically, which will protect the reader from the lies of this world and make accessible to him the reality of a beyond. Poetry which is assumed to proceed along these lines is usually called "visionary." And it is as a visionary poet that Crane is usually discussed.

This way of thinking carries with it a predisposition toward dogma. Interpretations of the unity of *The Bridge* and arguments about its success or failure as a visionary poem or as an epic derive from the unexamined belief that some Truth or Faith is needed to piece together our broken world; therefore, since Crane, like Blake and Shelley, wrote visionary poetry, he must be evaluated according to the efficacy of whatever vision the critic can find there. This evaluation has consisted, first, of attempting to subordinate everything in the poem to a few lines or to a single propositional statement and, second, of accusing Crane of having failed in communicating the truth he was aiming at, or of having partially succeeded in what was a great but impossible dream.

But the Romantic tradition in which Crane is writing has been profoundly antidogmatic from the beginning. In Crane's poetry the balance between circumstantial or contingent truth and its dissolution in random occurrence is never given over in favor of some answer from Beyond. Crane celebrates the possibility of meaning, faith, and work in individual circumstances, while he demonstrates through the dramatic contexts of the poems that "meaning" is a temporary product of an always creative-destructive mind. This is why seeing Crane as a "redeemer" must be seriously qualified. I do not believe that Crane's poems represent an attempt to reassert the religious consciousness in an unreligious age. Their honesty and skepticism continually see through the efforts of the mind to redeem the world. What Crane

Preface

has discovered is that the power of the mind never has depended on the absolute truth of its beliefs. Instead, the flexibility of the mind, its genius for disagreeing with itself, is its greatest strength.

This study begins with the origin of antidogmatic thinking, the Romantic revolution in sensibility. Specifically, I begin with the radically new ways of thinking Kant introduced into the modern world through his three critiques, and then I explore some of the implications these ways of thinking have had as important questions concerning human values have been asked in their terms. It is in the philosophy of Hegel that we find the fullest exploration of these questions.

In the *Phenomenology of Spirit* Hegel demonstrated just how unpredictable the world and man really are. And he eliminated the finality and authority of normative thinking. Furthermore I believe that writers in the Romantic tradition have come to terms with their own personal experience in ways analogous to his. They evolved, in effect, an anticulture from which they criticized the "realities" and "stable" values of Western civilization. By examining their own personal experience with painful honesty, they discovered the gap between the names of feelings and the feelings themselves. They recorded not only the stability of life, but also its chaos and its unmanageability. However, they were not nihilists. On the contrary, they discovered that the sense of value, the will to imbue life with meaning, is not a function of normative thinking at all, but follows from having the courage to face reality on its own unpredictable terms. Hegel, I believe, has given us a metaphysic for what we now call the Romantic tradition. And it is in the light of this tradition that the *Weltanschauung* of Crane's poetry emerges most clearly for us.

Acknowledgment

I have not attempted to cite every instance of my indebtedness to Morse Peckham, Distinguished Professor of English and Comparative Literature at the University of South Carolina. His radically behavioristic interpretation of the Romantic tradition provided the groundwork for this study of Hart Crane. I would like to thank Ennis Rees, A. E. Claeyssens, Edward Weismiller, Robert Ganz, Thomas S. W. Lewis, Nancy Hurley, and especially Les Barnstone for their valuable suggestions, and Della Becker for her help in preparing the manuscript. I cannot adequately thank Mr. James Dickey and Carol Malone.

VISION
of the voyage

1

Main Currents in Romantic Psychology

Romanticism is a relocation in thought which occurs when an individual is able to express what is undeniably real to him without invoking any authority beyond his own experience. Such an individual puts himself at odds with all forms of confirmation when he embraces the perversity of truth instead of the complicity of agreement. He takes on the responsibility not of pretentiously imagining what he cannot see, but of seeing what he could not possibly have imagined. Two beliefs sustain him in his Promethean task: first, in Hegel's words, that *"there is* nothing, whether in *actuality* or *in thought,* that is as simple and as abstract as is commonly imagined," and second, that it is better to appreciate experience for what it is than to gain compensation after refusing to do so. The freedom that is required for a Romantic to see his own experience as abundant revelation must be met with unscrupulous inventiveness in order for him to express what he sees. Then *our* task of understanding him, our relocation, begins.

What are the philosophical precedents for the Romantic's pursuit of the truth of his own experience? At what point in history did philosophers, concerned with questions about "truth" and "experience," begin to talk about individualized states of

Vision of the Voyage

consciousness? With the advent of Romanticism in the late eighteenth century, some philosophers became psychological, in the sense that they began to study the logic of the psyche. Hegel in particular was a revolutionary who explained how to regard the "external" world as objectifications of mind. And he explained how to regard subjective states of consciousness as objects which could be isolated and described. His *Phenomenology of Spirit*[1] (1807) is a philosophy of experience and a metaphysic for Romanticism.

A metaphysic describes underlying patterns of thinking, feeling, and acting. Religious beliefs, political opinions, and even commonly held assumptions about the nature of the physical world reflect an operative metaphysic. These various belief systems may be said to *police* individuals within a culture, since they define and perpetuate habitual behavior. Unquestioned beliefs are the real authorities of a culture. Therefore, if an individual can express what is undeniably real to him *without* invoking any authority beyond his own experience, he is transcending the belief systems of his culture. And he is literally expressing its underlying metaphysic in startling, revelatory ways. Paradoxically, by totally individualizing his own experience he is also universalizing it. He is expressing those patterns we all act out every day although we are insensitive to them because our minds are clouded by habit. Such an individual is a Romantic. He is also a "realist" of the first order.

If a Romantic is really evading the authority of habit in order to see the clear pattern of his own experience, the greatest disservice we can do him is to set him up as an authority in his own right. In this way we dogmatize his work by interpreting it in terms of the beliefs and opinions it embodies. We hope to redeem his work

---

[1]*The Phenomenology of Mind,* trans. J. B. Baillie (New York: Harper and Row, 1967). I also refer the reader to Walter Kaufmann's translation of the "Preface" in his *Hegel: Reinterpretation, Texts, Commentary* (New York: Doubleday, 1965), pp. 363-458. And I believe that Kaufmann's translation of the title, *The Phenomenology of Spirit,* is preferable to Baillie's.

from confusion by rendering it orderly and unified, but actually we drain away its life when we speak on its behalf. The content of a Romantic work of art does not possess the kind of order and coherence we assume a belief system does, because a Romantic work expresses uncensored patterns of experience. So we should approach an artist whose subject is his own experience by asking what unquestioned patterns of behavior it brings to light, not what opinions it defends. Every Romantic artist takes his life in his hands and dares to be a beginner in understanding it. Hegel prepares us intellectually to study such an artist. For he demonstrates that one can speak philosophically without speaking dogmatically. He shows us that the order we give experience by means of rational beliefs is superficial and, more importantly, that the deepest patterns of our lives, our metaphysics, are dynamic rather than static. They exist in the struggles of life and define themselves by their opposition to other patterns in a continuously problematical world.

Philosophically, Romanticism breaks away from the major assumptions of systematic thinking before Hegel. Thus we need to understand those assumptions in order to view Romanticism historically. However much earlier philosophers disagreed, their various attempts to formulate systematic explanations for phenomena and to disprove earlier explanations rested on the assumption that the world and language can be symmetrically related. That is, they thought that an explanatory system should be able to account for all processes of reality. They believed in the possibility of a *constitutive* metaphysic. Eventually, then, the philosophical endeavor, which would extend beyond metaphysics to every area of man's interests, should succeed in bringing him into a harmonious relationship with the universe. Therefore the task of the philosopher was to test for internal coherence and applicability what generations of thinkers before him had formulated. Always before him was the goal of a valid explanation which it was his calling to approach. Every error that he discovered in another's work or in his own was considered a

Vision of the Voyage

failure in as much as it delayed the realization of the ideal constitutive metaphysic.

The assumption of the possibility of such a metaphysic seems to have guided the very earliest thinkers. Consider, for example, the questions asked by the Pre-Socratics: What is the world made of? What is its cause? Thales suggested water; Anaximenes, air; and Heraclitus, fire. But the answers these philosophers arrived at are less important than the predisposition implied by their questions. They all agreed that the world should be knowable and that knowledge should have an internal coherence and unity. Furthermore, as these thinkers began to elaborate upon their answers, demonstrating how one generating substance produced through various principles of change the materials we live among, they strove for sophistication and refinement of argument, but always within a hierarchic explanation. Even the philosophers who were not monists, like Pythagoras, a dualist, and Empedocles and Anaxagoras, who were pluralists, were working in a similar way to reduce the diversity of their experience to a single coherent explanation. And the intellectually satisfying structure of that explanation was assumed to be analogous to the structure of the world they were attempting to describe.

We know very little about the Pre-Socratics beyond their interests in the physical world. But it is instructive that what statements we do have from them about society, such as those of Heraclitus on politics, are modeled on discussions of physical reality. Heraclitus obviously asked the same questions about the state, resting on those same assumptions, that he asked about the physical world. As he demonstrated in his discussion of the world-stuff fire, constancy is an illusion resting on an opposition of tensions. His dicta "War is the father and King of all," and "Strife is Justice"[2] extend his metaphysical formula to political

[2] Fragments 44 and 62, trans. John Burnet in *Early Greek Philosophy* (London: A. and C. Black, 1920), pp. 136-137.

concerns, thus broadening his whole explanatory system without violating its coherence. Seldom is a philosopher able to break completely away from his intellectual tradition and ask fundamentally new kinds of questions that result in an explanatory system radically different from the ones he already knows. More often he continues, by a process of analogy, to ask questions harboring the same basic predispositions of thought suggested to him by his teachers. And so, although his work may appear at the time startlingly original—Heraclitus' fire after Thales' water—, it is capable of little or no development beyond the scope of older systems.

In the philosophy of Plato, however, we find such a redirection of thought. It was precipitated by a crisis of skepticism in which the very possibility of knowing the world and of dealing with it responsibly was brought into question by the Sophists. It is important to understand how Plato, reinstating the goal of a constitutive metaphysic, answered the threat of moral disorder implied by skepticism. In this way we can appreciate both the strengths and weaknesses of dogmatic or pre-Romantic psychology.

The Sophists were professional traveling educators who took advantage of the surfeit of time and means in the new moneyed class in fifth century B.C. cities. They were "enlightened" rhetoricians who emphasized oratorical cunning and demogogic tactics as means toward political and financial advancement. Basic to their arguments were a subjectivism and a relativism of values profoundly opposed to the philosophical endeavors of earlier thinkers. Protagoras, for example, when he argued that "Man is the measure of all things,"[3] was perfectly willing to sacrifice the intellectual satisfaction of a hierarchic metaphysic if it impeded the far greater satisfaction of becoming wealthy and powerful. These men were not, we should notice, particularly

---

[3]John Burnet, *Greek Philosophy: Thales to Plato* (London: Macmillan, 1914), p. 111.

Vision of the Voyage

original thinkers who asked new sorts of questions and made people see the world in a new way; they were businessmen, not philosophers. In fact they based their self-serving arguments on the most fundamental questions asked by the other Pre-Socratics. In suggesting what the underlying substance of the world is, the earlier philosophers had used the word *physis*.[4] This word gradually came to mean what is real over against what is mere convention (*nomos*). And the Sophists used this very distinction in arguing for the subjectivity of values. The important point to realize, though, in connection with the Sophists is that their consideration of philosophical issues did not strive for consistency of explanation, even for a consistent skepticism. Their aim was rather to construe ideas in order to further their own extraphilosophical interests.

The work of Plato may be viewed in large part as a response to the egotistical skepticism of the Sophists. How does one meet the argument that "right" is only what is to one's advantage or that moderation is a virtue of the weak? Plato's solution to this problem, his theory of forms, incorporated in a sense the work of Parmenides (changeless universality—for Plato the "real" world) and Heraclitus (change—for Plato the world of appearances). But Plato's epistemology went far beyond an analogous treatment of the questions already asked by earlier philosophers. His achievement represents a profound redirection in the history of thought, and, as we well know, his work has provided the "generative ideas"[5] for centuries of further philosophical speculation.

But more important for our purposes than the sheer quantity of questions modeled on Plato's work is the underlying assumption—the possibility of a constitutive metaphysic—that

---

[4]W. T. Jones, *A History of Western Philosophy* (New York: Harcourt, Brace and World, 1952), I:61-62.

[5]A useful phrase suggested by Susanne K. Langer in *Philosophy in a New Key* (New York: The New American Library, 1951), p. 19.

he reinstated in philosophy. This assumption has continued to support and determine Western thought until the ideological revolution in the nineteenth century we will be most concerned with. Plato, Aristotle, the Christian Church, and early modern science reinforced in their own ways the assumption of the symmetrical relationship of language to the world for twenty-three centuries. It was mainly, I believe, Plato's brilliant epistemological strategy in his moral battle with the Sophists that reinstated this assumption and gave it the power and long life that it enjoyed. His strategy was to give to abstractions the most honorific and uncontested status—"reality." Furthermore, he expounded his epistemology, his solution to the problem of the one and the many, in elaborate metaphors emotionally charged. The myth of the sun and of the cave, the paradigm of the divided line,[6] and the way of ascent[7] succeed in establishing a hierarchy of values from self-seeking deception and appearances to the publicly real and knowable Good. Thus Plato created a metaphysic, an epistemology, and an ethic that were mutually dependent and supportive.

When Plato answered the skepticism of the Sophists as he did, he made morality—patterns of choice in thought and action—a matter of public debate, to be conducted in a vocabulary that transcended, it was assumed, individual circumstances. Thus, at the same time that Plato established in the minds of his students the necessity of a moral and intellectual responsibility beyond their most immediate interests, he also established the belief that all the interests of individuals within a society should be reconcilable. In this sense his *Republic* attempts to demonstrate that man can be at home in the universe. It now becomes clear what the "meaning" of the assumption of the possibility of a constitutive

---

[6]*Republic,* trans. Paul Shorey, in *The Collected Dialogues of Plato,* ed. Edith Hamilton and Huntington Cairns (Princeton: Princeton University Press, 1969), pp. 745 ff.
[7]*Symposium,* trans. Michael Joyce, in Hamilton and Cairns, p. 563.

metaphysic was for the ancient world; and the significance of that assumption remained basically the same, I believe, until the nineteenth century. Bearing in mind Plato's role as a teacher, arbiter of values, and founder of the Academy, and above all his concern for the chaos imminent in the Sophists' skepticism and subjectivism, we may say that the function of his hypostatized constitutive metaphysic was to establish a publicly acknowledged authority that would maintain and stabilize human values. In this way it helped to render behavior in society more predictable and controllable.

We should see how this assumption operates in terms of individual psychology. A member of society is faced, let us say, with a moral dilemma. He must choose to act after his own interests which conflict with a well-established value of society, or to act to the detriment of his interests in favor of the value. Seeing the value itself as "real" establishes for the individual a hierarchy of interests, so that it is to his *ultimate* interest to conform to the values of his society. He is then a good man. Of course, this is a simplification. The more intelligent a man is, the more complicated his decisions become. And the distortion those "real" values undergo through definition, legislation, and actual judicial practice is well known. The example of Socrates' death should be comment enough on the paradoxes this way of interpreting experience can produce.

Indeed, the figure of Socrates, *vis-à-vis* Plato, is very instructive not only concerning the metaphysical assumption we have been considering, but also concerning the mechanics of those important redirections of thought. For Socrates seems to have taught Plato how to break away from the philosophical limitations of earlier thinkers and ask new questions capable of great elaboration and refinement. And the method Socrates taught Plato can equally be seen, I believe, in subsequent ideological revolutions, particularly in the one we will consider in the nineteenth century. That method is irony, the strategy of responding to statements inappropriately. The purpose of irony is to establish a whole new semantic context with its own (the ironic strategist's) standards for appropriate responses. This is the method Socrates uses in Plato's dialogues to prove to the Sophists that they really know nothing. And Socrates masterfully avoids having irony turned back on himself by admitting that his wisdom lies in *knowing* that he knows nothing.[8]

This is tantamount to saying that any explanation can be destroyed by irony. The Sophists had used a similar strategy, of course, in their arguments, but without really understanding what they were doing; their immediate interests were their only concern. But Plato, fully schooled in the use of language by his teacher Socrates, not only understood this method of reasoning, but also saw how he could use it to prevent the moral chaos he saw imminent in the work of the Sophists. After catching his opponents in a web of semantic confusion, Socrates ultimately clarifies the issues in the dialogues by appealing to "self-evident" and eternal realities, the ideas. By always working toward more and more abstract abbreviations of the problems, Socrates makes the truth of the final concepts appear to be objective and immediately apprehendable to the unbiased mind.[9] The reality and the public accessibility of the values of society have continued to be the strongest argumentative authorities over individuals through the eighteenth century, and to a great extent through the present day.

It is not possible for us to follow all the various forms that the assumption of the possibility of a constitutive metaphysic took in the history of thought. But I have dwelled on its significance in the work of these early thinkers in order to emphasize the importance of this assumption, a cornerstone in Western philosophy, and to suggest what its function might have been from the beginning. It is the key, I believe, to understanding how lim-

---

[8]*Apology,* trans. Hugh Tredennick, in Hamilton and Cairns, p. 15.

[9]The best discussion of Socratic irony is Søren Kierkegaard's brilliant thesis, *The Concept of Irony With Constant Reference to Socrates,* trans. Lee M. Capel (New York: Harper and Row, 1965), p. 69.

itations were imposed on the infinite possibilities for behavior before the nineteenth century and, for all but a few, in the nineteenth and twentieth centuries as well.

Of course, it is with these few, the Romantics, that we will be most concerned. In their work we find evidence of a profound redirection of thought, but unlike any that came before, one that did not end by reinstating the assumption we have been discussing. No, the history of Romantic art is the history of the explorations of a few men who strived to comprehend their own experience without the assumption of the possibility of a constitutive metaphysic. Each generation of nineteenth and twentieth-century thinkers who form the Romantic tradition was faced with a unique set of problems left by its immediate predecessors. Again certain predispositions of thought were passed down; certain sorts of questions characterized and, to a large extent, determined inquiry into the nature of value. As a result, one finds it increasingly difficult, proceding in a chronological examination of this literature, to offer meaningful explanations for the issues involved without referring to the dilemmas in the very origins of Romanticism.

Those dilemmas revolve around the concept of value, the justification and, it is assumed, the impetus for behavior. Values, we may say, are categorical interpretations of experience which serve as directives for behavior, whether verbal or nonverbal. When the realization of a constitutive metaphysic, or when living and writing within the context of a metaphysic already assumed to be constitutive, was rejected by the Romantics, the notion of value had to be approached in a whole new way. The redefinition of value without a constitutive metaphysic was the task Romanticism undertook from the beginning.

The reasons for this undertaking and many of the difficulties it involves can be seen clearly in the work of Immanuel Kant. *The Critique of Pure Reason* (1781)[10] provided an epistemology

---

[10] Translated by N. Kemp Smith (London: Macmillan, 1929), second edition.

which freed the concept of value from its earlier metaphysical context. In that work and in *The Critique of Practical Reason*[11] and *The Critique of Judgment*[12] Kant demonstrated how to ask questions about value without, at the same time, asking questions about the "real" world. In a sense we may say that Kant undid all that Plato bequeathed to Western thought when he placed "reality," the *Ding an sich*, beyond the reach of man's mind. But in order to understand the redirection of thought Kant began, we need to view his philosophical endeavor, as we did Plato's, against the background of skepticism it attempted to answer.

Hume represented to Kant somewhat the same threat the Sophists did to Plato. Both were expounding skepticisms that seemed answerable only through radically new orientations toward the problems involved. And the implications of Hume's skepticism for science and for ethics were to Kant even more intolerable, I suspect, than the moral chaos Plato saw in the work of the Sophists. For the interests of Hume were not extraphilosophical like those of the Sophists; he was just as concerned as Kant was with the nature of values and ideals that seem to hold society together. But he also felt compelled to bring to light the full implications of Lockean empiricism for ethics as well as the unsoundness of this epistemology as a basis for science. I have suggested that the notion of a constitutive metaphysic served to stabilize the categories of value in a society by honoring them with the status of "reality" and thus to render behavior in the society more predictable and controllable; if this is true, it is particularly ironic that Hume's efforts to investigate man's grasp of reality should result in his frightening conclusions concerning the unreliability of our notions of cause and effect, induction, and even selfhood, which are the very foundations of the sense of value. No wonder Kant was "wakened from his dogmatic slumbers," probably with quite a jolt.

Kant's two aims in *The Critique of Pure Reason* were to

---

[11]Translated by T. K. Abbott (London: Longmans, Green, 1927).
[12]Translated by J. H. Bernard (London: Hafner Pub. Co., 1931).

vindicate science as a source of knowledge about the factual world from the skepticism of Hume and to find a basis for traditional moral insights beyond the purely physical world. He accomplished the first by suggesting that scientific knowledge was not knowledge of the *real* world (*noumena*), but of a spatio-temporal manifold (*phenomena*), the product of synthetic mental acts.[13] Scientific knowledge, therefore, is still viable, although greatly limited, since it is concerned only with this spatio-temporal manifold. And he accomplished the second by suggesting that moral judgments can also be viable, and in a sense sacrosanct, because they do not concern the spatio-temporal manifold. The eighteenth century's empirical orientation toward "reality," especially Hume's version of it, had drained that concept of any possible honorific application to values. Kant realized that from the point of view of his own transcendental logic, which provided the justification of scientific inquiry, statements about human values could no longer be modeled on statements about the "real world" or about scientific knowledge. His alternative was the concept of duty that he presented in the "categorical imperative."

But the most significant difference between this notion of duty and the one operative within what is assumed to be a constitutive metaphysic is that Kant's postulation was not adaptable by the authorities in society for policing purposes. And upon analysis this concept appears equally unsuited for purposes of self-control, imposing limitations on one's own behavior. Thus the formulation of the categorical imperative—" . . . I should never act in such a way that I could not also will that my maxim should be a universal law."[14]—reveals a number of difficulties. It rests on the assumption of a sovereign "good will" in an individual but provides no principle for adjudication between opposing "good

---

[13]Smith, pp. 698-714.

[14]*Foundations of the Metaphysic of Morals*, trans. Lewis White Beck (Indianapolis: Bobbs-Merrill, 1959), p. 18.

wills." In other words, it seems to set up a circular definition of virtue as the highest authority governing behavior and leaves the interpretation of virtue to the individual. As a result, Kant ends by asserting the need in a society for regularity of moral choice, but without suggesting how or even why that regularity might be possible.

What Kant called the categorical imperative was really a notion very similar to the notion of universal rights and duties on which the French Revolution had ideologically rested. And the fact that Kant could hold such ideas indicates that his sensibility had more in common with the Enlightenment than with the new age, although he formulated some of the ideas which would be most instrumental throughout the development of Romanticism. Still, the failure of the categorical imperative and similar ideas to serve the function of constitutive metaphysics defined the moral dilemma of Romanticism from its beginning.

The definition of value without a constitutive metaphysic was a different kind of moral dilemma from any that thinkers had faced before. How does one talk about the sense of value—one's most basic emotional and conceptual commitment—without talking about a stable "reality" or some authority external to one's self? The question obviously forces the thinker to take an ironic stance in search of a new orientation toward the issues. It should be apparent from the outset, then, that the elucidation of works of art in the intellectual tradition that explored this question should involve some difficulties not encountered in those of earlier periods. People are accustomed to receiving answers to questions, and when one is constructed so that no answer is appropriate, suspicions may arise about the worth of the question. Specifically, it could be argued that talking about value *means* talking about a stable reality and authority, and that trying to separate value from authority involves the question in a hopeless contradiction from the beginning. In this way some anti-Romantic critics have disparaged the whole movement on intellectual and ethical grounds. But the problems Romanticism deals with cannot, in my opinion, be so easily dismissed. Unless we are willing to accept some formulation of a constitutive metaphysic, we are forced to offer some explanation for the Romantics' approach to the problem of value.

Fortunately, that explanation has already been written: it is Hegel's *Phenomenology of Spirit*. Hegel brings to light, more clearly than they have ever appeared before, the issues at the heart of Romanticism. Far from being the most abstract and rarefied of thinkers, Hegel is really the most concrete and factual. He is immediately concerned with existential circumstances and the mental constructs with which they are managed. Thus his conception of Mind is not of an entity, but of the processes whereby categories are formed and dissolved in a reciprocal relationship with existential reality. What we are striving to understand in both the disciplines of introspection and history is, according to Hegel, the same: the limits of categorical responses in problem solving. When one idea is replaced by another or used in a new way in the recorded history of a culture or in the remembered history of an individual, we may be sure that a new set of problems is being defined. The interests of individuals and the exigencies of historical situations in their reciprocal relationships are the subject of the *Phenomenology of Spirit*.

The epistemology which Hegel devised to make analytical introspection and a philosophy of history possible rested on the conception of meaning as instrumental and tentative, instead of constitutive and final. Kant was on the right track, Hegel suggested, when he realized that previous epistemologies were naive in their dichotomy of man and the world in the relationship of knower to known. But demonstrating, as Kant did, that knowledge is actually of the categories of the subject and not of the inaccessible object created more difficulties than it solved. Hegel understood that whenever categories of thought are considered final, innate, or real, an impasse has been reached in philosophy, and indeed in all semiotic behavior. Thus his extremely subtle and unabashedly complicated discussion of the workings of the mind begins with an apology for being unable to set down the end the author had in mind or the position of the work on some subject as compared to positions of other writers.[15] Indeed, he later called the *Phenomenology* a "voyage of discovery"[16] and once we grasp his methodology we see it could be nothing else. For Hegel, unlike philosophers that preceded him, was less occupied with internal consistency and elegance in his explanation than he was with exploring the enormous complexity of human behavior, especially in its contradictory and paradoxical aspects. He could not have predicted in his "Preface" what he was going to find, because he was aware of and willing to admit the unpredictability of man.

The alternative to a constitutive metaphysic that Hegel gives us in the *Phenomenology* might better be described as a method than a system of philosophy. For it is an explanation about the process of explanation, and one that admits that all explanations become obsolete with time. In order to come to terms with Romanticism we must understand why this is so. Hegel pointed out that all articulate knowledge is categorical; that is, knowing the world means categorizing or objectifying it.[17] "Category" and "object" mean the same: a stimulus to which there are a

---

[15]Baillie, p. 67; Kaufmann, p. 368. We know that the "Preface" was actually written after the rest of the *Phenomenology*. So Hegel is here making an effort to preserve the sense of tentativeness and uncertainty, the unsystematic character, of philosophical enquiry, rather than attempting to conceal that character under an elegant apology.

[16]Kaufmann, p. 158. Kaufmann's favorite phrase to describe the *Phenomenology* is "the *Bildungsroman* of the *Weltgeist*."

[17]Baillie, p. 96. "Mind, however, becomes object, for it consists in the process of becoming an other to itself, i.e. an object for its own self, and in transcending this otherness. And experience is called this very process by which the element that is immediate, unexperienced, i.e. abstract—whether it be in the form of sense or of a bare thought—externalizes itself, and then comes back to itself from this state of estrangement, and by so doing is at length set forth in its concrete nature and real truth, and becomes too a possession of consciousness."

finite number of appropriate responses. In other words, knowledge is a process of limiting responses. Once this is grasped, it becomes clear why knowledge cannot be constitutive of reality, why it cannot remain stable through time.

All that time means to the individual is change of response. An individual is capable of coping with his experience only as long as he can distinguish one "moment" from another and remember a series of moments in chronological order. Otherwise he becomes confused, and action, both verbal and nonverbal, is no longer possible. In a sense, then, we may say that no two responses are ever "the same," or we would not be able to distinguish them. Of course, most of our categories, or objects of knowledge, represent a *range* of responses. Depending on our interests, if they are similar enough, we *call* them the same; thus, our mental lives may be discussed in terms of the categories into which we arrange our experience. However, to the extent that one is honest in introspection and astute in the study of history, he realizes that categories are extremely flexible. "Reality" seems hardly recognizable from one period of history to another and from one stage in a man's life to the next. What Hegel did in the *Phenomenology* was to demonstrate this flexibility.

Hegel not only pointed out the changes in the forms reality has taken through history; he also devised a way of talking about how these changes occur. Consciousness has, he said, two aspects, cognition and objectivity.[18] This amounts to saying that man knows and he knows that he knows. Thus every object of thought may be responded to as 1) an immediate manifestation of reality, or 2) a mediated construct of the mind. These are two attitudes we take toward our own experience, or two strategies we use in coping with it. They are also mutually exclusive; although a person may vacillate quickly from one to the other, he cannot, in the same moment, grasp his experience as both immediate and mediated response. Furthermore, every immediate response may

[18]Ibid.

become mediated, and every mediated response, immediate. Hegel called the principle at work in changing an immediate to a mediated response or *vice versa* "negativity,"[19] by which he meant the ability to group responses under a single categorical sign. For example, members of a set lose their individuality (they are "negated") when, for purposes of problem solving, only one point of similarity between them is focused on as definitive. Naming things, even just thinking about things, requires that we ignore a great deal of potential data. Selectivity is the key to problem solving.

This means that we pay a price for orientation, for what we call sanity. That price is the discrepancy between the conventional norms of response most of us call "reality" and all the possibilities of an organism's response with his environment, which seem to be infinite. Even on the most basic level of perceptual gestalt formation, the "meaning" of a configuration must be only one of a great number of possible ways the individual could respond to it. His normality depends on his ability and willingness to fashion his response on the validated models of his culture. It is the principle of "negativity" that makes policing of responses by a culture and ultimately by an individual possible. If one could respond only immediately to stimulus fields, their meanings would be fixed for him. He would then assume that his response was immanent in that field and thus completely determined by it. (This is, of course, the assumption of constitutive metaphysics.) But if he realizes that his response to a single configuration can vary greatly with time, he must then admit that the meaning of the configuration is not immanent in it, but instead is a matter of his own response and of the controls external to the configuration governing it.

---

[19]Ibid. "The dissimilarity which obtains in consciousness between the ego and the substance constituting its object, is their inner distinction, the factor of negativity in general. We may regard it as the defect of both opposites, but it is their very soul, their moving spirit."

Vision of the Voyage

We may say that the principle of negativity is what makes sign behavior possible. Of the various sorts of sign behavior, language is the most important tool man uses to control his responses. Indeed, every sentence with a subject and a predicate is a model of the process of mediation. When a predicate follows a subject there is a narrowing of the range of appropriate responses to both the subject and the predicate. And, on a more complicated semantic level, a conversation between two persons, each trying to grasp what the other means, continues until the categories used are mediated to the point where the interests of the two persons overlap. The *Dialogues* of Plato are excellent examples of the mediation of verbal responses for purposes of social control. But the difference between Hegel and thinkers before him is that he went beyond *using* the principle of negativity; he also grasped the fact that he was using it and just how.

One of Hegel's goals in articulating how knowledge works and in applying his epistemology to the history of thought was to demonstrate how one stops being victimized by ideas. People generally use language in vague yet dogmatic ways. Unequipped with the distinction between immediate and mediated response, they assume, when using categorical terms, that these categories describe some constant public reality. Argument is sustained and often carried to violent extremes because individuals believe that some final answer should be possible after every question. This assumption is a bequest of constitutive metaphysics and continues to motivate most people in their search for "the truth" and indeed for "themselves." Lurking in the background is always the disquieting feeling that something is wrong, but it is generally attributed to lack of information or is merely suppressed by systematic intimidation of one sort or another. Even Kant, who placed "reality" beyond knowledge, refused to accept the full implications of his epistemology for ethics. Instead he used the limits of knowledge, reaching the "antinomies" of reason, to reinforce traditional Enlightenment standards. Contradiction and paradox were for him indications that the mind had reached the limits of its power and must now be content to accept with humility the policing of the *status quo*. But Hegel realized that this attitude was viable only as long as the interests of the individual and of the policing powers of his culture were in some way reconcilable. Thus the individual may either establish the hierarchy of values mentioned above, so that it is to his ultimate interest to follow the norms defined by his culture, or he may be willing to accept a deviant status temporarily in order to evade those norms. However, if he is unable or unwilling to follow these strategies, his only alternative is to transcend those cultural norms. And this is what Hegel teaches the individual how to do.

Now we can see why Hegel is the key to understanding Romanticism. We find in the *Phenomenology of Spirit* a fully developed explanation, in epistemological and psychological terms, of the process whereby an individual undergoes and emerges from crisis situations. Hegel explains, in effect, how an individual redefines himself in a given cultural milieu by mediating his own responses. This is the essence of any "Romantic experience."

The "metaphysical" or "idealistic" bases of Romanticism have been often misunderstood, because the philosophical models for the discussion of Romantic ideology have been Platonic, Neo-Platonic, and even Aristotelian; whereas, the most important issues at the heart of this radically new way of conceiving the self in its world were formulated clearly for the first time only by Hegel. Thus talk about "another world," "ideal beauty," and the "creative imagination" hardly gets beyond paraphrase of the Romantics' own admittedly vague notions of what their poetry was about. No, what is needed is an explanatory system that can accommodate the new modes of objectifying experience characteristic of the nineteenth century, modes which were violations of what until then had been considered the rational, the wholesome, the sane. It is not surprising that the metaphor "organicism,"

Vision of the Voyage

used by A. O. Lovejoy[20] and Stephen Pepper[21] to explain Romantic ideology, should itself prove under analysis to be a profoundly Hegelian notion. In fact their explanations can be greatly clarified by referring to the *Phenomenology*. But we would do well to apply Occam's razor to much Romantic criticism and depend most heavily on a few central points of the *Phenomenology* for our main critical tools.

First of all, then, understanding that all propositional knowledge is the result of mediation and is therefore limited in its usefulness helps to explain the Romantics' quarrel with older criteria of "rationality." Even the law of noncontradiction became obsolete in light of Hegel's objective or pragmatic idealism. And Enlightenment definitions of right-mindedness were acceptable only as long as the individual was willing to accept personally the results of the enforced categorical interpretations of experience. In the late eighteenth and early nineteenth centuries, however, we find a number of poets who were not willing to accept those limitations and who set out to conceive their experience in a whole new way, a way, it seems clear, that was based on epistemologico-psychological insights most accessible to us now in their formulations by Hegel.

The most fundamental of these insights was the abandonment of the distinction between stimulus and response which characterized empiricism in the previous century. As the role of mediation in cognition and perception was increasingly realized, the "meaning" of the "external" world began to appear problematical. But it would be wrong to call the Romantics' revolt against empiricism "subjectivism," just as it would be wrong to call it "objectivism." Rather their approach to the problem of knowledge was to explore the interdependence of subject and

---

[20]*The Great Chain of Being* (Cambridge: Harvard University Press, 1961), p. 288 ff.
[21]*World Hypotheses* (Berkeley: University of California Press, 1948), p. 28 ff.

object, as Hegel said, by examining "knowledge as a phenomenon."[22] Thus otherness (the property of being an object) is itself a function of the mind, a way of responding to a stimulus field. Therefore it makes sense to speak of the existence of something, or its meaning, only *vis-à-vis* a knowing subject in a given cultural situation. And "subject," or "self," now has two meanings which we should be careful to distinguish: one is the sense of continuity one has through all his experiences (what Hegel meant by "cognition" as opposed to "objectivity") and another is the self-as-other,[23] all propositional knowledge of what one is like. It makes sense to speak of the latter only in terms of the cultural milieu out of which it arises. Furthermore, the self-as-other has two dimensions, a publicly recognized and defined role identification and the individual manner in which it is carried out. Now we may see why the distinction between stimulus and response had to be abandoned. "Stimulus" means some gestalt defined as an other, an object, but the perceptual-cognitive act is itself a matter of response. In other words, there is a contradiction involved in imagining an uninterpreted stimulus. Since "stimulus" means a finite number of responses defined as appropriate in a given situation, talking about "external" objects is really a way of talking about one's own responses.

Formulating the stimulus-response problem goes a long way toward clarifying some of the most important issues in nineteenth-century poetry and fiction. The Romantic lyric may now be seen as a representation of experience without the stimulus-response distinction. The empirical bias which had characterized earlier thinking no longer controlled the poet's investigation of his own processes of perception and cognition. As a result, poets increasingly realized that orientation was an

---

[22]Baillie, p. 135.
[23]See George Herbert Mead, *Mind, Self, and Society From the Standpoint of a Social Behaviorist,* ed. Charles W. Morris (Chicago: University of Chicago Press, 1947), p. 158.

Vision of the Voyage

emergent of goal-directed behavior. As Hegel said, "Reason is purposive activity."[24] Therefore, a suspension of goals radically alters "reality" for the individual. Thus when the Romantics stopped respecting the verbal and nonverbal goals assumed by constitutive metaphysics to be the poet's rightful directives, the "world" became for them something wonderful and mysterious. Since the meaning of experience was no longer seen as ontologically antecedent to it, no limitation on that meaning was justifiable. If a feeling, however unorthodox, was experienced, it should be acknowledged and investigated, for it was as real as the stone Dr. Johnson had kicked. The full implications of the conception "meaning equals response" (or "existence precedes essence") were to be realized in lyric poetry only gradually. But for each poet the strategy for exploring his experience was basically the same. The suspension of previous directives that had defined the poet's work made it possible for him to see hitherto immediate responses as mediated (contingent upon many factors, especially upon his will). Then he was able to focus clearly upon those feelings which emerged as his new immediate responses. The feelings a poet encountered as he experimented with his own objective reality became the subject of lyric poetry.

We can now appreciate the function of nature in the early nineteenth century as a source of knowledge and inspiration. First recall, though, that the moral dilemma which Kant's epistemology created but that his ethics, in my opinion, evaded was how to deal with the sense of value, the feelings that are assumed to underlie choice, without a constitutive metaphysic. What explanation can be offered for value if "reality" and a system of social control analogous to that "reality" does not support it. Kant, of course, placed moral responsibility and whatever "ultimate" knowledge man can experience in the noumenal self, which was tantamount to stopping all inquiry into the matter, for no more can be said about this source of intuition than about the

---

[24]Baillie, p. 83.

Ding an sich. But Hegel's approach to knowledge was capable of much greater development than Kant's, and it was one like his that the Romantics followed. Hegel's suggestion was to consider the sense of value phenomenologically.

This the first Romantics did by turning away from the categorical definitions of value enforced by their culture and by trying to experience and record the sense of value with relentless scrutiny as it occurred to each personally, alone. Nature was for them an environment that could be dissociated from civilization and from those publicly recognized values. Their first efforts in this mental adventure, especially Wordsworth's, were modelled on traditional religious experience; indeed, the vocabulary and tone of religious ecstasy have characterized much of Romanticism to the present day. But discussing the Romantics' "religion of nature" or their pantheism is little help in explaining why they turned from traditional formulations of good and evil to their own *Sehnsucht,* or vague longing, and passionately individualistic Divine enthusiasm, which were far from amenable to the norms of a Christian community. That sort of discussion also fails to account for the poetry later in the century that we feel needs to be called "Romantic" but that clearly has nothing to do with pantheism. Therefore we would do well to avoid relying on the apologies of the early Romantics for our own critical vocabulary. It makes considerably more sense to say that nature, and later in the century art objects and individual personalities, provided the Romantics with perceptual-cognitive fields relatively untouched by the official interpreters of value in their culture. Thus nature could be experimentally employed to examine something that un-Romantic, or un-Heglian, people accepted as absolute and unquestionable—the sense of value.

The Romantics realized that beauty, goodness, inspiration, all "spiritual" realities are objects in the sense discussed above. They are "realities" in the same way physical objects are realities: they are mediated responses whose meanings are not immanent in the objects but dependent on the expectations and

Vision of the Voyage

training of the perceiving individual. Consequently these objects are not fixed but may change their meanings for the individual depending on his needs and interests.

The recorded experience of various forms of ecstasy is an important Romantic phenomenon, which we may now describe in Hegelian terms. Such an experience is the creation by mediation of an important category of value, whereby responses are limited and given a single objectivity. This category is further identified by some configurational sign, taken from nature, say, that may elicit a similar response in the future. And perceptual data are rigorously filtered through this category, so that the experience is continued and for a while reinforced. But such an experience is necessarily short lived. Indeed the very effort to sustain ecstasy finally destroys it. For no two responses are ever really the same—repetition itself adds a factor each time—, so the sheer weight of diversity breaks up the category and the happy feeling is lost.

We find a similar situation in the Romantics' occupation with the processes of creation, especially with the ebb and flow of poetic inspiration. It is less important, though, to decide whether their poetry was as "spontaneous" and untutored as they liked to think, than to appreciate the meaning of the theme of spontaneity in their poetry. Upon introspection Wordsworth and Coleridge decided that they were passive in the creative act, that no amount of craft could produce great art without the poet's losing his own sense of control over what he was creating. In Hegelian terms this amounts to saying that there exists in the poet's culture no formulation of the experience he is having on which he can model his own rendering of it. Previous objectifications of longing and rapture had always served some constitutive metaphysic, and thus expressed socially approved or condemned emotions. However paradoxical these feelings may have appeared circumstantially, their meanings were assumed to be public, not private, realities. Who would ever have thought that a poet would one day create a whole new feeling, derived from the examination of what

Main Currents in Romantic Psychology

"feeling" is? But this is what the Romantics did. Their *Sehnsucht* was the feeling resulting from focusing mentally on the discrepancy between the public "meaning" of some configurational sign or natural object and all the possible responses that they knew personally one could have to it. No wonder their poetry was vague, and significantly so! For their solutions to this unique poetic problem—how to express what had never been expressed before—were either to take material from older literature (such as medieval ballads) and use it in a new way, for their purposes, or to create from heretofore "nonpoetic" material a whole new Romantic symbology.

In both cases we find the revolutionary practice, which was to begin a whole poetic tradition extending to the present day, of using obviously symbolic images and scenes without suggesting in the poem what their interpretation should be. In this way it is implied that they are somehow explanatory in themselves, but that the only way the reader can know their meaning is to undergo himself the poet's experience that lies behind them. This is the meaning of Coleridge's statement that a symbol "always partakes of the reality which it renders intelligible."[25] Coleridge's formulation of the synthetic "Imagination" was an attempt to explain how cultural innovation occurs, how new conceptions of reality become part of the poet's culture. The feeling of passivity that accompanies this innovation, the feeling that some truth is being communicated from a high source through the poet, is a substitute for the authority and validation of the poet's culture. The special kinds of *Sehnsucht* and rapture I mentioned were entirely unjustifiable in terms of the poet's culture, but at the same time they were expressions of the most important and deeply felt values that the poet experienced. The function of the highly honorific concept of the "Imagination," and the Divine authority which was felt to validate it, was to create a basis for an

---

[25]*The Statesman's Manual* in *Biographia Literaria*, Bohn's Standard Library (London: G. Bell and sons, 1905), p. 343.

Vision of the Voyage

anticulture composed of poets and thinkers exploring matters the larger culture would not condone. Thus the new Romantic symbology, the use of the "meaningful meaningless,"[26] became the special vocabulary of these mental adventurers; it was to separate and protect them from the "Philistines."

Alienation, then, was the price the Romantics paid for cultural innovation. Alienation, which in the broadest sense is a result of a consistently ironic stance toward the values of one's culture, is at least as old as Socrates. It would seem to be a large part of the psychology of any thinker beginning a redirection of thought. But the character of Romantic alienation and the irony on which it was based differed in one important respect from that of all previous revolutions in ideas. That is, Romantic alienation is not a temporary crisis that an individual passes through on the way to a more satisfactory social adjustment. Neither is it a temporary strategy for success in argument. This kind of alien, once he has fully grasped the epistemology I have been discussing, can never again look at his society's formulations of value without being aware of their inadequacy. Therefore, unless he is willing to embrace some constitutive metaphysic and label his mental and emotional experiments in the psychology of value as deviant, he must remain, to a large extent, alone and unsupported by the authorities of his culture. As a result he will probably seek some reinforcement from other Romantics, and thus strengthen the movement and propagate it by encouraging a younger generation of aliens.

In this way there emerged in the nineteenth century a new intellectual role, fostered and maintained in an anticulture, whose occupation was the criticism of the norms and value formulations of the larger society. This the anticulture accomplished by developing a self-transcending metaphysic, a theory of reality that is never final, but whose categories are always open to

---

[26]See Morse Peckham's discussion of meaning in his *Victorian Revolutionaries* (New York: George Braziller, 1970), p. 265 ff.

correction and transformation by existential fact. The purpose of this self-transcending metaphysic was to cope with crisis situations which arose when categories of value, assumed to be constitutive of reality, could no longer accommodate the changing world. Only a group of thinkers who were themselves uncommitted to their culture's norms, who were more interested in what knowledge is than in which knowledge is "right," could have begun this criticism.

The history of Romanticism is thus the history, to use an important phrase from Nietzsche, of the "bad-conscience of society."[27] And it is a fascinating study because, as a solution to a cultural dilemma, Romanticism was astoundingly revolutionary. Never before had thinkers found themselves in the paradoxical position of introducing value into a culture by destroying for themselves what had been considered the basis of value. The epistemological revolution that made the criticism of culture possible also destroyed constitutive metaphysics. In other words it became necessary for the Romantic alien to live in a meaningless world in order to make meaning real again for his readers. He was a very curious priest.

It might be argued that the early Romantics certainly did not live in a "meaningless world," that their poetry was indeed the communication of the profoundest "constitutive" truth on which the world and man are based. Certainly their poetry often presents itself in just such a prophetic role. But it is easy to confuse the models for the expression of Romantic experiences—religious mysticism—with the actual function their psychological experiments may now be seen to have had. This is a crucial point in evaluating the importance of the first stage of Romanticism,[28] which was much involved with hopes for the

[27]*Beyond Good and Evil*, trans. Walter Kaufmann (New York: Random House, 1966), p. 137.
[28]See Morse Peckham's "The Dilemma of a Century: The Four Stages of Romanticism" in *The Triumph of Romanticism* (Columbia: University of South Carolina Press, 1970), p. 41.

Vision of the Voyage

perfecting of man and society. It has often been said that these hopes met with failure and that the next periods of nineteenth-century thought, "realism" and "naturalism," were opposed to the earlier visions. On the contrary, the hopes of Romanticism to redeem the world were, I believe, its least significant aspect, although its most conspicuous one. Critics have dwelled time and again on the "priestly" role of the Romantic poet and the hope his "spiritual" vision offered mankind. But most of these statements are based on the Romantics' own evaluation of their place in society. And two important aspects of their poetry demand that we qualify that evaluation a great deal.

The first is that the Romantics were always as interested in the dissolution of the sense of value as they were in its "ultimate reality." In much of the most powerful Romantic poetry these two themes are finely balanced and equally convincing: "Lines Composed above Tintern Abbey," the "Intimations Ode," "Ode on the Departing Year," and "Ode to a Nightingale," for example. One of the most endearing characteristics of Romanticism is the relentless honesty with which poets treated the experiences most important to them. Their phenomenological examination of the sense of value demanded the suspension of the tempting distinction between illusion and reality. It would have been easy enough to establish a dogmatic Romanticism that would have had much in common with the earlier long tradition of Christian poetry. In that case, the "truth" of the particular value formulations of the Romantics would have taken precedence over the contingency of value in general, and Nature could have been defended as the only source of inspiration. In that way they would have created another constitutive metaphysic. But the Romantics consistently refused to accept any experience of the sense of value as complete and final and so created a self-transcending metaphysic instead.

The second aspect of Romantic art that highly qualifies its "priestly" function is related to this distrust of dogmatism. It is the absence in their proselytizing and reforming literature of any definite program for social and personal redemption. The Romantics focused instead on the *principles* of reformation, specifically on the two aspects of change—destruction and rebuilding. This is one reason that much of Victorian nonfiction prose is, on first encounter, so puzzling. Often Carlyle, Arnold, and Ruskin are not really proposing cultural alternatives to contemporary dilemmas; they are, rather, fashioning elaborate metaphorical models of the process of cultural change. The central chapters of *Sartor Resartus* compose such a model.

Of course there is an important sense in which the early Romantics did think they would be able to point their culture toward cures for personal and social ills. I believe they thought that society, or rather each individual member of it, could operate in terms of a self-transcending metaphysic. Indeed, it is easy to see why the impossibility of that dream was not immediately apprehended. Grasping Hegelian epistemology is a thrilling experience in itself; the sense of power and control accompanying it is quite intoxicating. And there is nothing about this epistemology which suggests that the great majority of the members of a culture could not learn to use it. But that simply did not prove to be the case. Perhaps the best explanation we could offer is statistical. The large majority of people in Western culture since the nineteenth century have continued to function psychologically with various forms of constitutive metaphysics, while a few have separated themselves and evolved a metaphilosophy, which allows them to serve as critics of the larger culture.

Any student of Romanticism knows that no poet is consistently metaphilosophical. The need for security and reinforcement will occasionally result in an "Elegiac Stanzas" or an "Eolian Harp." And there is no reason to condemn the Romantics for being less than supermen in their ability to sustain alienation and a consistently ironic stance toward their culture and toward themselves. It would be more correct to say that Romanticism is not a description of certain men at all, but a description of a way of behaving,

Vision of the Voyage

as it is reflected in particular documents that have survived since the nineteenth century. We group these documents together and call them "Romanticism" not because of "qualities" they have in common or even because of the frame of mind we sense behind them. No, their similarity emerges only when we view them against the larger culture out of which they grew. All these documents share a common focus on the discrepancy between the formulation of the sense of value and the experience of it. Such a focus demonstrates the uniqueness of responses in a temporal sequence and shows how order, meaning, and value are defined in a culture by the selection of certain ranges of responses as normal and good and how these are strictly policed.

If this notion of the origin of value is correct, it should not be surprising to find that within a given culture the structure of value formulations is not hierarchic, with the categories of value exhaustive and mutually exclusive, but that values are often conflicting. Indeed Hegel demonstrated in the *Phenomenology* that every value measured against all the existential circumstances with which it could logically be expected to cope eventually results in contradiction and paradox. Therefore a strict policy of fidelity to the value formulations of one's culture will very likely end in some crisis situation. An individual functioning in this way may find himself vacillating frantically between systematic lying and moral panic. Romanticism is the study of those crisis situations and the psychological strategies through which an individual overcomes them.

The artistic means of examining the sense of value in this way is necessarily individualistic and "self"-centered, for the responses that are being weighed against the public formulations of them are above all unique. Similarly language, or the categorial resources the poet finds in the larger culture, proves to be inadequate for his purposes of expression. The high value attached to innovation in art begins here in the poet's striving to create for his unique responses unique sign-equivalents in the work of art. Since language itself is highly selective and structured, he experiments with various sources of discontinuity, first within the accepted limitations of usage, then within new limitations he creates for himself. There are three reasons, then, for the Romantic artist's generation of a unique style: as a language the Philistines cannot understand, it alienates him from his larger culture; as the poet's own set of value-formulations, it sustains his identity and gives life its "meaning"; and as a perceptual-cognitive experiment, it allows him to isolate, examine, and criticize the value formulations of his larger culture.

This brief look at the foundations of Western philosophy and at the beginnings of Romanticism in light of Hegel should indicate something of the boldness of this redirection of thought which began in the nineteenth century. The astonishing rate of artistic innovation we have seen since then, as well as much of the character of modern art, are traceable to the problems defined by Romanticism from its beginnings. Alienation and irony, the anatomy of crisis, a contextual perspective for knowledge, the primacy of style, all have played important parts in the shaping of modern poetry, and all derive from the problems involved in examining the sense of value phenomenologically. Of course other thinkers, notably those in the wasteland tradition begun by T. S. Eliot and his followers in the New Criticism, have mourned the death of constitutive metaphysics as the source of a uniquely modern poverty in religion, philosophy, and poetry. And positivists, believing that *all* metaphysics are dead, continue to denigrate Hegel, or what he means to them. But strongly opposed to both these currents of modern thought is the continuing tradition of Romanticism. I would like now to turn to the poetry of Hart Crane, one of the most profoundly Romantic sensibilities the twentieth century has produced. For we can see there, in one of its most brilliant forms, the intellectual tradition that is an alternative both to Eliot's school and to the positivists, and that is today a vital stream of Western thought.

2

White Buildings:
The Character of Crane's Lyric

In his letters and essays Crane tried to explain his intentions as a poet. These statements need interpretation, because, like those of the earlier Romantics, they seem maddeningly unhelpful as explanations for poetry, and, worse, because these statements have been made the basis for almost all criticism of Crane's specific works. The "essential unity" of *The Bridge*,[1] its success or failure as a "Myth of America,"[2] the worth of a "logic of metaphor"[3] have been centers of attention in Crane criticism.[4] But these concepts were never, properly speaking, "explanations" at all. We would do better to call them "justifications" or "apologies" and recognize their limitations in light of the circumstances under which they were formulated. Like Coleridge's

---

[1] See Crane's statements to Herbert Weinstock in a letter dated 22 April 1930. *The Letters of Hart Crane 1916-1932*, ed. Brom Weber (Berkeley: University of California Press, 1965), p. 350. Hereinafter cited as *Letters*.

[2] Letter to Otto Kahn, 12 September 1927. Ibid., p. 305.

[3] See Crane's essay "General Aims and Theories" in *The Complete Poems and Selected Letters and Prose of Hart Crane,* ed. Brom Weber (New York: Liveright, 1966), p. 221. Hereinafter cited as *The Complete Poems.*

[4] See the essays in *The Merrill Studies in "The Bridge,"* comp. David R. Clark (Columbus: Charles E. Merrill, 1970).

White Buildings: *The Character of Crane's Lyric*

statements on imagination and Wordsworth's on nature, Crane's theories about his art grew from important ulterior motives, the least of which, however, was exegesis.

Before looking at Crane's most famous and enigmatic dicta, we should consider some general statements on the nature of poetry which he made to Gorham Munson in a letter dated 17 March 1926. In that letter, which is perhaps our best introduction to his Romanticism, Crane explains why his poetry cannot be expected to express a coherent philosophical position and to support an ethic. His explanation clearly reflects a distrust of the constitutive use of language found, for instance, in science as well as a firm belief in the poet's immunity to the value formulations of his culture. For Crane, the poet's chief responsibility is to be true to his own experience and to find some way of articulating it.

> Poetry, in so far as the metaphysics of any absolute knowledge extends, is simply the concrete *evidence* of the *experience* of a recognition (*knowledge* if you like). It can give you a *ratio* of fact and experience, and in this sense it is both perception and thing perceived, according as it approaches a significant articulation or not. This is its reality, its fact, *being*. When you attempt to ask more of poetry,—the fact of man's relationship to a hypothetical god, be it Osiris, Zeus, or Indra, you will get as variant terms even from the abstract terminology of philosophy as you will from poetry; whereas poetry, without attempting to logically enunciate such a problem or its solution, may well give you the real connective experience, the very "sign manifest" on which rests the assumption of a godhead.[5]

What he calls the "sign manifest" of experience is remarkably close to what Coleridge meant by "symbol." Compare Crane's cryptic elaboration, poetry "give[s] you a *ratio* of fact and experience, and in this sense it is both perception and thing perceived," with Coleridge's definition quoted in Chapter 1,

[5]*Letters*, p. 237.

Vision of the Voyage

"The symbol always partakes of the reality it renders intelligible." In both statements the distinction between stimulus and response has dissolved. What the poet writes about, the "thing perceived" or "reality," is no longer distinguished from his own personal experience. In other words, all "objects," in the "external" world or in the mind, are seen to be organized responses. Therefore all interpretations of reality can be said to be equally acceptable ontologically. Here Crane is following the earlier Romantics in realizing that the status "reality" is mainly an honorific concept used for social and personal control. When Crane sets himself apart from science, with its enormous intellectual prestige, and from all other attempts to describe the world systematically, he is at once rejecting constitutive metaphysics and accepting the Romantic stance of irony toward his culture.

It is interesting to notice in this letter that Crane places Plato alongside modern science insofar as both recommend themselves on the basis of the "truth" of their explanations. However Crane states that Plato's worth lies in the degree to which experience is *organized* in his works and has nothing to do with the "intrinsic truth" of his system.[6] Crane points out that Plato banned poets from his Republic because they posed a threat to his interpretation of reality. Constitutive metaphysics, we may say, has traditionally required muscular as well as logical defense.

It has long been an influential notion, asserted by historians of ideas who are quite willing to accept an instrumental definition of truth, that some periods of history have achieved a more coherent, well-defended "synthesis" of thought than ours today, and enviably so. But Crane asserts strongly in this letter that he is not interested in delineating any such system for his time. This is an important point, for it suggests not only that Crane refused to identify with any constitutive metaphysic, but also that he did not cultivate the utopian and redemptionist hopes we noticed in the

---

[6]Ibid., p. 238.

works of earlier Romantics.[7] Crane was not, that is to say, a transcendentalist.

I believe that, although such hopes certainly sustained the early Romantics, redemption was not the *raison d'être* of their art: alienation for the study of the sense of value was. If we can avoid confusing these two explanations, we may be able to grasp Crane's poetry and to understand exactly what he shares with earlier thinkers. The letter to Gorham Munson takes us the first important step, indicating the extent to which Crane identified with the original Romantic dilemmas and the most important ways he diverged from them. He accepted the awesome burden of examining his own experience, fully realizing that it would never be reconcilable with the value formulations of his culture. But he also undertook this task, aware that the ecstasy of transcending values must be short-lived and, finally, that it is no more "real" than the various emotions which policed the values of his culture. Here is the explanation for the extreme fluctuation between euphoria and despair in Crane's life and art. Most importantly, though, Crane consistently avoided making either of these states of mind definitive of his endeavor as a poet. Carrying the honesty of the Romantics in introspection further than it had ever gone, he faced and recorded the inevitable failure of his own "language experiment."

We should notice that, in general, later nineteenth- and twentieth-century poets who base their work on the fundamental Romantic problems sometimes sound very much like transcendentalists. The familiar prophetic tone of Whitman and Emerson often rings loud in Crane. But if redemptionism functions chiefly to sustain the Romantic artist in the absence of support from his culture, then this should not be surprising. When later Romantics, like Crane, feel compelled to justify their efforts to others or to themselves they often point in the vague direction of

---

[7]See also Crane's reply to Weinstock, "God save me from a Messianic predisposition!" Ibid., p. 350.

the future, toward the hope new conceptions of value may hold. And indeed they always do offer hope. For isn't a large part of "hope" the expectation that, within a given problem situation, some interpretation may resolve the discordant interests? And since the number of interpretations, or ways of responding to the situation, are infinite, a solution in the form of a hypothetically "right" interpretation always remains a possibility. Therefore in times of frustration, energy may be channelled away from the various attempts to resolve the problem in favor of some interest and toward this refreshing possibility, which involves no tension, just as it solves no problem. Redemption was the form hope took for the Romantics.

It is a mistake, though, to place too much importance on Crane's prophetic image of himself. This self-conception, when it operated, and his concern for the "spiritual" potential of America are much less interesting and significant than the psychological explorations he carried out in their name. Redemption certainly need not be a cornerstone for an interpretation of *White Buildings* or *The Bridge;* in fact, since the concept served as a respite from problem solving, it actually detracts from the issues at the heart of Crane's poetry. This is well illustrated in some notes Crane published under the title "General Aims and Theories"[8] in which he mixes the platitude derived from Eliot that our age is spiritually bankrupt and his own transcendentalist self-encouragement with some penetrating comments on the real subject of his poetry, the individual's experience of value. Crane felt that the symbols of past mythologies exist for the poet in the same way that the symbols of contemporary secular experience do. It is pointless to discard them as archaic and equally pointless to ascribe esoteric meaning to them. Crane does not follow Eliot into disillusionment. For he insists that the poet, in spite of feeling unsupported by a metaphysic, concentrate on rendering honestly and fully his own feeling states, whatever they are. In

[8]In *The Complete Poems,* p. 217 ff.

White Buildings: *The Character of Crane's Lyric*

this way, he says, "a poet will accidentally define his time well enough simply by reacting honestly and to the full extent of his own sensibilities to the states of passion, experience and rumination that fate forces on him, first hand."[9] Viewed against his poetry, this statement comes closer to describing Crane's accomplishments than any of his high-sounding defenses written to Otto Kahn or Yvor Winters. If we can understand what Crane means by "define his time" and by "reacting honestly," we should be able to penetrate most of the difficulties of his style. For his verbal experiments were solutions to problems he faced in these two endeavors.

Crane saw himself as an "absolutist,"[10] and we must be sure to understand why. He did not mean that his poetry was an attempt to approximate some perfect and eternal set of values which can only partially be rendered into language. (That is what Gorham Munson and others *wanted* him to mean.) No, what Crane meant by "absolute" is quite close to what Hegel meant by the same word.[11] The last chapter of the *Phenomenology* is called "Absolute Knowledge," by which Hegel means apprehending experience, whether one's own or someone else's, with a full awareness of what knowledge is. The individual who is able and willing to grasp that *he* is a number of constructs which have meaning only in problem situations is in a privileged position compared to less knowledgeable members of his culture. For he can examine his own experience (or "himself") as a cultural emergent. He can understand his own limitations in ways that would be too painful in ordinary circumstances. We may say that a person reaches absolute knowledge when he changes an immediate response (unself-conscious experience) to a mediated one, with the interests at work in selectivity revealed.

[9]Ibid., p. 218.
[10]Ibid., p. 220.
[11]Baillie, p. 797. "This last embodiment of spirit—spirit which at once gives its complete and true content the form of self, and thereby realizes its notion, and in doing so remains within its own notion—this is *Absolute Knowledge.*"

Vision of the Voyage

Crane's poems work toward a revelation which could be characterized as seeing through an experience without surrendering or demeaning a naive sense of its reality. Absolute knowledge for him is a momentary recognition of what is naive about the experience *and* what is wonderful about it. Such a recognition is absolute in the sense that it is both undeniably real and free of the biases of the poet and of the reader. Crane accepts the problematical nature of its interpretation and the precarious state of its existence as challenges to expression.

In order to understand Crane's societal role as a Romantic poet, or as an absolutist, we should put "absolute knowledge" in behavioral terms. As we have seen, the immediate responses of individuals within a culture are strictly policed by various forms of intimidation and reward. The most important of these is the use of explanation, which I would like to call the false mask. This is the use of language to obscure, rather than to clarify, the interests at work in a problem situation. It should be apparent why "mask" will not describe a pseudoexplanation: the best explanation anyone could construct might justifiably be called a mask, since it is a construct which distorts and simplifies perceptual-cognitive data. In this sense, Carlyle's philosophy of clothes might as well be called a philosophy of masks. But I am concerned here with another use of explanation, the kind that directs attention away from the interests at work in problem situations so that the problems are sustained.

An individual's patterns of behavior require considerable energy to be changed. First of all, certain immediate responses have to become mediated: an explanation must be constructed that identifies the interests at work in the behavior pattern. This identification allows the individual to suspend those responses. Then, if he is strong enough to delay the rewards in the old pattern and to endure the punishments that inhibited his changing the pattern previously, the individual may adopt the rewards and punishments of a new problem situation, one amenable to the interests he now wishes to hold. Needless to say, if all individu-

White Buildings: *The Character of Crane's Lyric*

als were constantly undergoing these severe crisis conditions, their society would be dangerously unstable. Therefore it is not surprising to find that language is rarely used to create such value-suspending situations. By far the most numerous explanations constructed in a society are those which reinforce patterns of behavior.

We must be careful not to become dogmatic in our understanding of "interests" at work in given problem situations. An "interest" is a construct in an explanation and must not be mistaken for a force "in the world." Also, due to the fact that data and interpretation are always changing (every response is unique), "interests" are always hypothetical. Still, it is important that we distinguish an explanation that can be used to restructure responses so that a problem situation may be replaced with a new one, from an explanation that maintains a current structure of responses and thus the old problem situation. Hegel demonstrated that the only significant meaning of "freedom" was the former use of language. And it seems particularly apt to interpret freedom as the penetration of a mask, for an individual changing some pattern of behavior must see the interest he focuses upon as previously hidden. His new interpretation of the elements in the old problem situation must seem to him to be a penetration to the truth. Like the idea of "redemption" or "hope" the concept of "mask," which plays such an important part in Romantic thinking, is chiefly a means of encouragement in problem solving. Or, as in Melville, it becomes an agonizing puzzle, when the thinker becomes aware that interests are *always* ulterior: uncovering one mask only yields another. We may say that an "interest" is a hypostatized cause behind an immediate response, an interest being imagined to be a distinct reality. It is useful in mediating the response, so that some undesirable pattern of behavior may be changed. But since a new set of immediate responses is the goal of this type of introspection, the honest individual will emerge with the disquieting feeling that a new hidden interest which he does not understand lurks beneath his present actions. Then he

Vision of the Voyage

has gone only halfway toward "absolute knowledge"; when he is able to accept every interest he has or thinks he might have as a construct for self-control and the definition of value, then he will have reached absolute knowledge, and he will be fully "free," but only temporarily.

Strictly controlling this freedom and making it unattainable for most people is the false mask, which also harbors the metaphor of penetrating appearances to ulterior interests beneath. However, the interests formulated by this kind of explanation only solidify the current structure of responses, so that any change in behavior becomes increasingly difficult. Constitutive metaphysics has provided the most influential models for the creation of false masks in every area of human behavior, the chief one being the sovereignty of logic. The assumption that all one's responses are ultimately explainable in some way provides a relief from the tensions involved in the continuous process of categorization and problem solving. But, at the same time, when an "interest" is not only defined, but also justified and honored with some validational label like "real" or "natural," the behavior pattern supposedly deriving from that interest will be reinforced. Similarly, defining the interest as "deviant," "sick," or "evil" also serves to impart a greater reality to a pattern of behavior than it deserves, so that it also is reinforced. A firm belief in the "truth" of categorical signs and in any set of rules for manipulating them (such as those we call "logical"), makes the individual search anxiously for some name for his behavior. Since any categorization, whether laudatory or deprecating, is preferable to ambiguous, contradictory, or uninterpreted experience, he will commit himself to a tortured, monotonous existence rather than face the chaos of his own experience.

How does a writer penetrate the false masks of language, and, as he becomes increasingly aware that all knowledge is mask-like at best, how does he proceed in the interpretation of his experience? By creating a unique set of categorical signs for the symbolization of experience, the Romantic poet is able to focus

White Buildings: *The Character of Crane's Lyric*

on the discrepancy between his immediate responses and the common formulations most people accept as the real name and essence of them. In this way he is able implicitly to criticize the value formulations of his age which others take for granted. In other words, he penetrates the false masks of society. Furthermore he alienates himself from his own experience. By examining his own immediate responses phenomenologically, he focuses on those "interests" within himself on which the very reality of his world rests. He comprehends the "objectivity" of his experience; he understands why reality has for him the shape it has. Then he continues to explore and record the limitations of his world, approaching the point at which his own constructs fail to cope with the existential facts they must confront. Crane's poetry often touches the brink of chaos: it is as heroic as it is terrifying. Thus the double-edged epigraph from Rimbaud for *White Buildings, "Ce ne peut être que la fin du monde, en avancant."*

We find in *The Bridge* the fullest exploration of the limits reached by a sensibility as it is systematically stripped of all its false masks. But before turning to that work, Crane's "growth of a poet's mind," we should look at the shorter lyrics published together in 1926 as *White Buildings*. We can see clearly there the strategies for alienation, introspection, and the removal of masks that Crane employs later in *The Bridge*. These strategies rely on the double conception of self worked out by the early Romantics and expressed philosophically in Hegel's distinction between cognition and objectivity. In fact, we may say that the central theme of *White Buildings* is the illusory nature of the self-as-object and of its propositional world. Perhaps the best introduction to this theme is a short meditative lyric in which these two concepts of self—as construct and as undifferentiated process—are juxtaposed.

It is appropriate that Crane selected "Legend" to open *White*

Vision of the Voyage

Buildings, for the subject of that poem is really the epistemology on which all the psychological explorations that follow are based. This poem employs the kind of symbolism described above as the "meaningful meaningless." That use of language, recall, was a solution to the problem the early Romantics faced when they attempted to describe subjective states for which no explanation existed. Their solution was to create a verbal configuration, usually a series of metaphors, for which no explanation existed. If the reader acquiesces to these metaphors, he will become disoriented ideologically, and if he continues using them to reinterpret his own experience, he may be led to disregard the categories of value ordinarily at work in his culture in favor of new ones held by other members of an anticulture. He will then have, to use the phrase of Wallace Stevens, a "new knowledge of reality."

In this poem Crane is redefining metaphorically the individual's orientation toward the past. The false mask here examined is the responsibility one feels to interpret experience in terms of the validational categories of his culture. It is very difficult to resist the tendency of memory to blur and distort onrushing experience, especially as it becomes increasingly distant in the past. Indeed the exigencies of problems with which one is immediately concerned seem to require that distortion. Certainly if one is to play a role successfully, even a deviant one, he must remember aspects of his past which substantiate that role and explain away or forget others. But Crane is suggesting that there is an alternative to judging the past according to the demands of some conventional self-construct. And since all experience may be said to reside in the past (the present is the past as soon as it is apprehended or objectified), this alternative really applies to all experience. The alternative is a highly disciplined insouciance, an ironic attitude characterized by indifference to the emotional interpretations accepted by most people as the "meaning" of phenomena. And since accepting conventional interpretations of one's experience is the chief means of adopting a role-construct

White Buildings: *The Character of Crane's Lyric*

for oneself, this attitude is profoundly alienating. It therefore requires that the individual accept some counteridentity to sustain himself.

"Legend," then, sets forth the epistemology for the whole Romantic endeavor.

> As silent as a mirror is believed
> Realities plunge in silence by . . .
>
> I am not ready for repentance;
> Nor to match regrets. For the moth
> Bends no more than the still
> Imploring flame. And tremorous
> In the white falling flakes
> Kisses are,—
> The only worth all granting.[12]

Crane posits three metaphors, a moth consumed by a candle flame, snowflakes kissing the earth, and a reflection in a mirror, to suggest the sovereignty of phenomena over conceptualization. The sheer diversity of responses to any experience eventually makes any orientative construct of it obsolete. Knowing this is to apprehend reality clearly, coldly, as inherently meaningless. And as the world is seen in this way, the ground for any conventional self-construct is swept away. There can be no responsibility, no "repentance," in a sensibility whose only interpretational criterion is lucidity. Crane acknowledges in the third and fourth stanzas the difficulty of this endeavor, especially as it amounts to a radically new perspective on one's own past. Introspection must now take on a disinterested objectivity, and no conceptualization of what one is like may be allowed to solidify and act as a principle of selectivity in the interpretation of experience. Therefore in this kind of introspection one must return again and again to the facts of his life, the random stream of occurrences, in search of the interests which have determined the "meaning" of his experience. This process is what Crane means, I believe, by

---

[12]*The Complete Poems*, p. 3. Subsequent references are to this edition.

Vision of the Voyage

the "bright logic." And the final metaphor, "step/The legend of their youth into the noon" is virtually equivalent to the penetration of masks.

There are, of course, a number of interesting questions we should ask about the approach to experience defined by this poem. These are explored by the other pieces in *White Buildings*. "My Grandmother's Love Letters," like "Legend," is a poem about the past; in a sense it is also about historiography. Is it possible to recapture the meaning of a past event, even with the help of surviving documents? This poem suggests the difficulty and the futility of such an attempt. Trying to understand what those letters might have meant to the poet's grandmother is obviously a Kafkaesque problem. But more importantly, even if one succeeded, the result would be at best only a momentary appreciation of someone else's beautiful illusion. In the last lines even the "meaning" of the rain shifts, mocking the poet's efforts.

> And so I stumble. And the rain continues on the roof
> With such a sound of gently pitying laughter.

In order to pursue the "bright logic" defined by "Legend," one must give up the notion that the meaning of the past is accessible and public. It is instructive to notice that significant changes in a well-established behavior pattern, through cultural revolution, for example, or through psychotherapy, are always accompanied by a reinterpretation of the past. Some old formulation of what in fact occurred is replaced with a new "truth" which justifies the changes. The theory of social contract replaced that of the divine right of kings. "Progress" replaced "the fortunate fall." If one is to achieve absolute knowledge, or reach the point where any behavior pattern may be changed, he must be willing to reinterpret the very nature of categorical thinking and relegate every proposition to the status of "illusion," even the proposition of his own being. Crane is, I believe, concerned with this kind of reinterpretation of experience. And the first step in pulling away the most cherished false mask of Western man, which presents

White Buildings: *The Character of Crane's Lyric*

the individual as an entity persisting through time, is to dissolve the "substance" of the past. This is exactly what Crane has done in "My Grandmother's Love Letters." Just as he gives up the attempt to judge the past in "Legend," here he gives up the attempt to respond emotionally to it in the appropriate way. Both poems are assaults on a deeply engrained mental habit which most people equate with sanity: the imposition of a consistent fiction upon the past.

Fiction begins, of course, in the "present" moment of apprehension; how can a poet successfully reveal that moment as a mask? His only tools consist of language itself—more categories, more masks. Does the problem involve a hopeless contradiction? No, the paradoxical nature of the Romantic endeavor only bears out the conviction that the criticism of culture, or the correction of cognitive models for behavior, must be an endless process. Obviously no correction is final, so each poet's contribution to this endeavor must eventually reach the limits of its usefulness. It is then another generation's task to find some new way to cast the highly valued concepts of its culture in relief against relentless fact. The continuing search for new styles in the history of Romantic art has been the method of coping with this problem. This search has been a series of experiments extending the frontiers of the meaningful meaningless. New ways must constantly be found to express the intimate patterns of our lives.

The basis of cultural innovation is metaphor, of which the meaningful meaningless is an application. Usually, however, when one organizational construct replaces another, the transition between them is masked by the notion of "discovering the truth." The new construct is soon taken for granted, just as the old one was, and so no discrepancy is imagined between the new explanation and the reality on which it is imposed. A simple example of this process is the *idiom,* like "running stream," whose metaphoric character is seldom appreciated. More complex organizations of knowledge into scientific and philosophical systems may also be seen as elaborations upon basic metaphors. To the extent that the organizational construct is confused with the process of reality it describes, one may be said to be victimized by the metaphor.[13] But the important difference between the Romantic meaningful meaningless and other forms of metaphor is that the former resists the tendency to be confused with the world it describes. With the help of paradox, synesthesia, and other seemingly contradictory juxtapositions of images, the Romantic use of metaphor actually sustains and focuses upon the tension between an organizational construct and the reality it interprets.

The reader encountering this use of language is forced either to reject the metaphor or to cultivate a new set of perceptual habits especially for this poetry. If he chooses the latter, he will be performing a kind of psychological experiment in which he can observe his own process of disorientation and readjustment. The highly protected situation of reading poetry is free from the cultural restraints which would inhibit change as well as from the rationalizations which would mask it. There an experiment such as Crane's *dérangement des sens* is possible. This amounts to an exploitation of the unlimited ambiguity of sense experience. It forces the reader to change the "meaning" of a perceptual gestalt or to create one he has never experienced before purely on the basis of association, that is to say, without the mask of some explanation. The conclusion such an experiment points toward is that the only basis of human behavior is imitation or action by analogy. The value of this final explanation lies not, of course, in what it tells us, which is very little, but in the new set of questions it allows us to ask. We abandon the search for a basis of behavior and of identity, and we examine instead the process whereby behavior and identity change. The method Crane uses in this examination may be explained as the self-induction of crisis.

We begin to see how this occurs in "Sunday Morning Ap-

---

[13]See Colin Murray Turbayne's discussion of this process in *The Myth of Metaphor* (Columbia: University of South Carolina Press, 1970), pp. 26-27.

White Buildings: *The Character of Crane's Lyric*

ples." The majority of false masks, defining interests which stabilize behavior, are functions of various social roles; their whole purpose is the maintenance of those roles. Therefore, the way to penetrate them is to estrange oneself somehow from the roles they support. Only the alien can recognize the platitudes and sentimentalities of his culture for what they are. But what role must the alien then play? We have discussed the Romantic artist's counteridentity, one which he and his colleagues respect in the absence of support from the rest of society. But I am concerned here with the very basic habits of perception and categorization which most people take for granted all their lives and which they would feel perverse tampering with. How does one penetrate these primary illusions, the objects and feelings of his world? In this poem Crane suggests that one adopt the role of art-perceiver in nonartistic situations in order to achieve the necessary irony—as one going to an art museum is prepared to accept perceptual reorientation. Replacing any role with that of art-perceiver causes the "meaning" of phenomena to become highly fluid. Looking at "life" as if it were "art" and vice versa is a basic strategy of alienation and disorientation. It plays an extremely important part in all of Crane's poetry.

"Sunday Morning Apples" is a poem about the artist's prerogative to disorient himself and others by the creation of a personal style for apprehending reality. The first two stanzas suggest the power such a style may exert over the perception of nonartistic phenomena.

> The leaves will fall again sometime and fill
> The fleece of nature with those purposes
> That are your rich and faithful strength of line.
>
> But now there are challenges to spring
> In that ripe nude with head
>   reared
> Into a realm of swords, her purple shadow
> Bursting on the winter of the world
> From whiteness that cries defiance to the snow.

Vision of the Voyage

By "style" I mean a set of principles governing the selection and arrangement of details in any art object, or for that matter, in any perceptual field. Fully grasping the style of some artist amounts to learning how to respond to any perceptual field in terms of his principles of selectivity. Crane is interested here in this tendency of life to imitate art. The intensity and beauty of William Sommer's paintings represent a challenge to nonartistic reality, or to the art-perceiver who would see the world as strikingly as Sommer does. The boy in the third stanza, I presume, is not in a painting, but he is perceived as if he were, as a configuration of light and shape. The secrets tossed to the artist by the apples of the fourth stanza are his uniquely Romantic talents for apprehending reality in ways his society would call "mad." The madness, spiritual drunkenness, and destructiveness with which Crane so gleefully ends the poem define in terms solidly from the Romantic tradition the artist's act of inducing perceptual confusion, which is the first step toward restructuring reality on the demands of a new style.

> I have seen the apples there that toss you secrets,—
> Beloved apples of seasonable madness
> That feed your inquiries with aerial wine.
>
> Put them again beside a pitcher with a knife,
> And poise them full and ready for explosion—
> The apples, Bill, the apples!

Furthermore, this process is considered an "inquiry," a perceptual experiment in which the apprehension of reality, whether artistic or nonartistic, is discovered to be a function of style.

We may now see that those "interests" I spoke of earlier, the various masks and false masks that define reality for us and constitute the problems which are our mental lives, are "styles" of behavior. Furthermore, as the Romantics discovered, if patterns of behavior are to be profitably explored the search for a *basis* or constant explanation for behavior must be abandoned in favor of a phenomenological study of changes in those patterns of

White Buildings: *The Character of Crane's Lyric*

behavior. Seeing this process in terms of "style" goes far beyond trivializing behavior; it suggests an artistic model for understanding the complex patterns of meaning we must somehow unravel to begin to see human actions clearly. Adopting the art-perceiver's role toward phenomena, we see that our knowledge consists of constructs forming complicated sets of illusions that make problem solving possible within contexts much larger than the misleading knower-known. I believe that Crane's experiments in the poetic lyric may be profitably seen as attempts to express this insight. It is one of the cruelest ironies of literary criticism that the difficulties of Crane's poetry, whose direction is entirely toward lucidity, should be labelled "obscure."

Perception, then, the recognition of the world categorically, is possible only on the model of some style, a principle of selectivity. Maintaining a given style amounts to identifying with it, accepting it as a social role and a self-definition. In order to change that style, and thus the character of reality, one must adopt an ironic role, for Crane the art-perceiver's. Lucid observation of the transfiguration reality undergoes as Crane suspends his notion of who he is defines his lyricism. This suspension of self can best be appreciated in "For the Marriage of Faustus and Helen" and the six "Voyages." But before turning to those and the other difficult longer poems of *White Buildings* we should look briefly at the other short lyrics.

We saw in "Sunday Morning Apples" how the character of an experience (the boy running before the sun) may be changed by modeling one's response to it on another set of responses "inappropriate" to the situation. Now we see in "Garden Abstract" that it is possible to respond to a situation exclusively or obsessively in terms of one style. It is not terribly important whether the overwhelming response being described is sexual or aesthetic. What is interesting in the experience is the loss of identity (the sense of separateness or otherness) felt by the woman as she makes one pattern of response the *only* meaning of the experi-

Vision of the Voyage

ence: "And so she comes to dream herself the tree." The nearest analogue to this situation might be momentarily falling in love with an extremely charismatic personality. The intense gratification of excluding all responses foreign to one tyrannical model sustains this ecstasy or insanity. I mentioned a similar psychological phenomenon in discussing the earlier Romantics' ecstasy in Nature. The only requirement for this experience is that no immediate problem-solving be demanded of the individual, for, as in the states of euphoria or despair, no goal-directed activity is possible with a single rigid interpretational construct. Indeed since identity is, I believe, altogether a function of goal-directed activity, the loss of memory, fear, and hope in the poem amounts virtually to immobility.

"Stark Major" makes a nice companion piece to "Garden Abstract," for it treats a converse theme, one that necessarily follows from the ecstatic experience—the encroachment of unsympathetic responses upon the exclusive one so that the intense feelings of oneness are lost. Crane returns to this theme repeatedly: the loss of meaning or emotion in an experience through the fragmentation of it. In "Stark Major" the poet is observing his own actions and addressing himself in the second person. He seems to be one of the two lovers in the first stanza, but he immediately separates himself not only from the situation he was involved in, but also from the very idea of himself defined by that situation. Like "Legend" and "My Grandmother's Love Letters," "Stark Major" studies the consequences of a cultivated irresponsibility toward the past. The poet dissociates himself from his former role as lover; it is the death of that role, then, that is referred to in the first line. From that point on, the experience which had been a coherent single reality breaks apart. Interestingly, it is the light of day which begins this process. The lover belongs to the world of darkness and dreams, but when the poet rejects that role the elements of his experience lose their old meaning. He sees the color and shape of his beloved under the

White Buildings: *The Character of Crane's Lyric*

bedclothes but interprets no responsibility there for himself. She calls to him, but he hears only the laughing accusation of his own footsteps and then interprets her calls as faint good-byes.

> And she will wake before you pass,
> Scarcely aloud, beyond her door,
> And every third step down the stair
> Until you reach the muffled floor—
>
> Will laugh and call your name; while you
> Still answering her faint good-byes,
> Will find the street, only to look
> At doors and stone with broken eyes.

He looks at the world with "broken eyes," because his life has lost its redeeming illusion of coherence and objectivity. Hers has not; therefore, her memory is greater. It still holds her pains and joys together in a single fiction. The poem is composed in "stark major" (major keys are affectively "bright," minor ones "dark") to express the violent effect of clarity upon experience. We will see that approaching the clear understanding of a situation for Crane often means threatening cherished feelings associated with it.

This is well illustrated in two other short poems, "Pastorale" and "In Shadow," both dealing with the poet's ambiguous attitudes toward an uncertain past. In "Pastorale" the poet again addresses himself and leaves the question suspended whether the unfortunate past could have been otherwise.

> I can only query, "Fool—
> Have you remembered too long;
>
> Or was there too little said
> For ease or resolution—

Could more interpretation, more words, have resolved the situation happily, or is one a fool even to ask? The question is not "Could the past have been otherwise?" but "Is such a question meaningful?" We find here more fragmentation as the poet

Vision of the Voyage

questions his nostalgia, so uncomfortable among a few violets, leaves, and the wind.

"In Shadow" is no more resolved. We are not allowed to know the fabulous lady's answer. Notice, though, that she and her answer belong to that well-protected world of night and dreams. The poet plainly enters that world to approach her, and he cannot safely bring her out of it. Like the ecstasy of "Garden Abstract" and the lover in "Stark Major" (and like La Belle Dame of Keats and Tennyson's Lady of Shallot), this woman's significance for the poet is a delicate affair and must be protected at high cost. Notice, too, the part played in this poem by style, as I defined it earlier.

> Out in the late amber afternoon,
> Confused among chrysanthemums,
> Her parasol, a pale balloon,
> Like a waiting moon, in shadow swims.

The experience is narrated as if it took place in the extra-artistic (or so-called real) world, but it is apprehended only under the strictest perceptual conditions—as if the experience were a work of art. We might say that the cognitive model for the experience is an impressionist painting, in which a single configuration categorizes chrysanthemum, parasol, balloon, and moon. The poem's heavy rhyme and assonance reinforce this sense of stylization. However, strict stylization tends either to drift toward obsession and immobilization or to break down under the pressure of one's own varying responses. In the last stanza the poet tries to save the experience from the increasingly severe stylization of encroaching darkness but refuses to tell us if he succeeds.

> "Come, it is too late,—too late
> To risk alone the light's decline:
> Nor has the evening long to wait,"—
> But her own words are night's and mine.

The problematic conclusion, like that of "Ode to a Nightingale" or "Ode on a Grecian Urn," is most important and revealing.

White Buildings: *The Character of Crane's Lyric*

The attempt to redeem experience by thought (by subsuming object within subject or exhaustively categorizing all of life) must be suspended just as the temptation to break down all categories into chaos must be withstood. The discovery that we think in illusions is no reason to stop thinking.

A serious problem is beginning to form now as experience is considered in these terms. What sort of limits does one place on the apprehension of reality once the functions of negativity and perceptual style have been grasped? This is a question which held diabolical fascination for Crane. He imagined in "North Labrador" a condition of absolute stasis in which responses never change, in which reality is constant. It is significant that Crane did not (in the next to last line) identify such a state with "death," which is itself a categorical response involving a propositional, objective world.

> No birth, no death, no time nor sun
> In answer.

No, this state represents the failure of the mind to categorize reality altogether. It is the only alternative to illusory knowledge, which is the best we have. Crane was acutely aware that there is no escape from categorization. His frame of reference never includes a "beyond," and his "vision" is always limited to existential situations.

Crane's rejection of what Hegel called the "false infinite"[14] was a source of great anxiety for him. There is no propositional knowledge, no category of the understanding, to which one may legitimately have *final* recourse. Like the eyes of the damned in Sartre's *No Exit,* the poet's eyes must remain forever open to the

---

[14]See Hegel's *Science of Logic,* translated by A. V. Miller (New York: Humanities Press, 1969), p. 137. " . . . the main point is to distinguish the genuine Notion of infinity from spurious infinity, the infinite of reason from the infinite of the understanding; yet the latter is the finitized infinite, and it will be found that in the very art of keeping the infinite pure and aloof from the finite, the infinite is only made finite."

Vision of the Voyage

reality in which he finds himself. We should bear this in mind while reading "The Fernery," which grapples with just this predicament. There the poet confronts a pitiable situation, an old woman nearly blind. But his treatment of it, again in the second person, amounts to a consideration of his own responses. Similar to "In Shadow," this poem presents a visual experience highly controlled by a style of perception. And again light functions at the end of the poem to threaten that style and thus the meaning of the experience. In the first six lines Crane focuses on the components of the visual pattern, but he allows us to see an awful reality beneath this aesthetic surface. Then in the last four lines, when light changes the visual patterns, he admits the confusion and anxiety which he feels in his self-conscious position of observer. The last line suggests that he finds no escape from or redemption for the scene before him.

"The Fernery" breaks down a piece of categorical knowledge (the sick old woman), revealing it to be an "illusion," but then returns to that knowledge as inescapable. Thinking vacillates continually between analysis, which refines data, and synthesis, which generalizes it. But there is no third alternative, unless it is the stupor of "North Labrador," and there is no rest from the process. Categorization, illusion-making, goes on continually. So which illusions one accepts and moves among are forever problematical, open to change, and utterly without "justification." "The Fernery" represents the poet examining his own responses as he realizes he must remain trapped in this process.

Crane's determinism is quite different from the *que sera sera* variety, which is no more than a false mask for the status quo. Crane is less interested in *which* categories are unavoidable than in the fact that categorization itself is unavoidable. One can never merely *be*; he must be *something*. This epistemological fact of life, rather than civil injustice, lies behind "Black Tambourine." Thus the "world" referred to in the second line is not simply a bigoted society, but culture and its *modus operandi,* categorical definition. Whatever interests, ambitions, and desires the Negro

White Buildings: *The Character of Crane's Lyric*

in the poem may have, they cannot operate freely, without regard for the limitations imposed on him by his own particular set of cultural definitions. These are "illusions" certainly in the sense discussed above, but they represent no less of an impasse for him. In lines three and four the gnats seen within the confines of the bottle's shadow and the roach across its crevice are analogues for the Negro's situation. There is no point here of injustice, but merely a picture of a structured reality which, although it could easily have been otherwise, enforces its own limitations ruthlessly. In the second stanza Aesop represents the intelligent man aware of his own confinement (recall his deformity), who attempts to redeem the world by thought, but who does not ultimately affect any change in it. His most ingenious categorical model (Heaven) is reduced finally to words scattered in the air over his grave. Consistent with the use of light imagery in other poems we have examined, darkness represents in the last stanza categorical knowledge largely uncorrected by random data. This black man lives in a world of inescapable self-definitions symbolized by his tambourine and by the African carcass. The poem is a study, then, of the psychological prison which is the social role.

One might think that such a preoccupation with the categorical nature of knowledge and with its limitations in the midst of experience would produce a clinical poetry at odds with any humanistic tradition in literature. This is, of course, not the case with Crane. We can best begin to appreciate the place of empathy and love in his poetry by looking at his elegy to Ernest Nelson called "Praise for an Urn."

The poem begins with a strongly stylized memory of Nelson, incorporating his appearance, his origins, and what he meant to Crane. His personality, which Crane admired and identified with, is unforgettably expressed in the last two lines of the first stanza, (These lines were to be Crane's epitaph.)

> The everlasting eyes of Pierrot
> And, of Gargantua, the laughter.

Vision of the Voyage

The eyes of Pierrot are sad for his own plight and for the world he sees, but inspired by the moon, in love with art. The laughter of Gargantua is hungry, robust, and self-assured. Crane's memory of Nelson is highly selective, serving to create a myth around which the rest of the elegy revolves.

The second stanza recalls the conversations between Nelson and Crane which built this myth in Crane's mind. Nelson taught Crane how to respond as a Pierrot and as a Gargantua and thus how to cope with the difficult problems he would have to face. These conversations about death and the life of the mind are introduced by an image which draws on a whole tradition of Romantic speculation about the Imagination. Especially after the allusion to Pierrot in the first stanza, the "slant moon on the slanting hill" suggests (like Yeats' "The Cat and the Moon") the mutually transforming relationship of thought and reality. Stanzas three and four raise the question, then, what significance does the death of an individual have for a Romantic? We have seen Crane in several other poems treating memory constructs of "the past" as illusions and perhaps as illusions which victimize him. Here he is writing about the memory of a cherished friend; what is his attitude?

First, Crane has not abandoned his strictly existential orientation and his awareness of the limitations of knowledge. In fact, this poem is not about Ernest Nelson at all, but about Crane's memory of him. Crane never confuses the two in the poem, and in this way he avoids sentimentality. Crane and Nelson were both concerned with questions about what endures through time and what perishes. And they knew that the crematory clock commented both on their questions and on themselves. What, therefore, does remain? The answer is "what the dead keep, living still." In other words, what remains to us of the dead is what we have learned from them, how we remember and mythologize them. Time relentlessly destroys meaning and simplifies memory: responses must eventually lose their saving illusion of continuity. The poem does not offer any consolation for this fact.

White Buildings: *The Character of Crane's Lyric*

Utterly without regret, Crane recalls a friend who could view his own approaching death with the same objectivity with which Crane would celebrate his memory.

The elegy is founded on the willingness Crane and Nelson shared to accept the nothingness beyond categorical knowledge. The ultimate breaking apart of categorical thinking, of Crane's memory of Nelson (we find again fragments—gold hair, broken brow), and of Nelson's existence as a recognizable individual are symbolized by "the dry sound of bees/Stretching across a lucid space." The last stanza is particularly poignant, since it demonstrates the same willingness on Crane's part to surrender the illusion of substantiality even of this elegy. We see light used in the last line in a now almost predictable way. Lucidity, freedom from illusion, the "bright logic," and now the sun, all break down categorical knowledge. All meaning must ultimately be lost, since all meaning is illusory. This elegy is a testimonial from one man who held this belief to another.

We find in "Chaplinesque" a consummate treatment of these psychological strategies which Crane identified with Nelson, but which were inherited really from the whole Romantic tradition. The clown figure, which fascinated Laforgue, Mallarmé, and Cézanne, derives, of course, from the early Romantic alien. His costume and antics, which often barely conceal his aching heart, are signs of his ironic stance toward his culture, and they supply a stylized substitute for a validated social role. Far from being a straightforward entertainer or professional clown, he actually pities or hates those who laugh at him. He is an eloquent ironist. But we should not mistake him for the transcendental alien. For the clown has no hopes of redeeming society, and he is as ironic toward himself as he is toward others. The life he has made for himself and the mask he wears are, in a sense, ridiculous. For he is aware that there is no escaping the basic predicaments common to every man. His humorous and devious response to the burden of this knowledge gives the clown figure a unique flavor of pathos.

Vision of the Voyage

Like the lines describing Nelson, then, the figure of Chaplin defines a kind of Romantic myth which describes the poet's plight in the world and his response to it. The confrontation of the poet (Crane generalizes Chaplin into "we") with hostile forces, symbolized by the policeman, is inevitable, as is his ultimate defeat. That is, not only must a poet writing in the Romantic tradition be willing to receive disdain from a society which asked for no criticism, he must also face the eventuality that his poetry will change nothing. The powers of society, which are necessarily brutal, uncompromising, and insensitive to the poet's esoterica, represent a real threat to the poet's identity, to his own mental equilibrium. So "Chaplinesque" defines the dangerous and, in a sense, impossible situation in which the poet finds himself. His response is complex, for it involves contempt but not withdrawal. Chaplin's evasion of the city cop is always temporary, and the two inevitably meet again. Furthermore, in the fourth stanza Crane insists on qualifying even the contempt. He refuses to accept the status of public enemy, rejecting any interpretation of his behavior as a lie or a scheme. This is understandable, for the whole point of irony is to avoid the interpretations that one is offered. The poet must evade the policing forces of his society without accepting the deviant labels applied to him.

By means of this ironic stance the poet can still "love the world" and let the "heart live on." One is reminded of "The Rime of the Ancient Mariner," when the mariner blesses the watersnakes and the albatross drops from around his neck. In "Chaplinesque" the feelings of tenderness toward the kitten and the transformation of the ashcan correspond to the mariner's revitalization. For both Coleridge and Crane emotional spontaneity and imaginative vitality are indications of success in the Romantic artist's attempt to transcend the value formulations of his culture. It is important, therefore, that in this little myth of the poet in society, the Chaplin figure be more than a roguish sad clown. He must succeed at and be genuinely gratified by some-

White Buildings: *The Character of Crane's Lyric*

thing which his society cannot understand. In this way the poet will be able to sustain himself emotionally, not succumbing to the policing forces of his society, but confronting them, criticizing them constantly.

"Chaplinesque" is an instructive piece to study in order to understand how Romanticism as an intellectual tradition came into the twentieth century. The earlier transcendentalist elements are there, but they are used for new purposes. The imagination has been dissociated from any hope of redemption and now serves to create and maintain protective styles of behavior in a hostile or brutally indifferent society. The counteridentity of the Romantic alien, as seen in the Chaplin figure, has incorporated a flexibility and a capacity for irony greater, I believe, than it ever enjoyed before. And an awareness of the mask-like character of knowledge has been fully accepted so that the bitterness of disillusionment has been transcended.

The Romantic lyric has always depended in large part on the poet's willingness to suspend categorical notions of who he is in order to experience phenomenal reality in terms other than those defined and policed by his culture. At the stage of Romanticism represented by Crane's poetry, this suspension of role identification, as we see in "Chaplinesque," is so thoroughgoing that no unquestioned self-definition remains to sustain the poet. He may be able to generate styles of behavior which can protect him from society and behind which he can carry on his relentless program of irony and the criticism of value formulations. He may be able to transform reality in art and to experience the gratification of controlling his habits of perception to the point where his feelings become crystal clear and divorced from their societal determinants. But in the process he becomes terribly vulnerable. Categorical self-definition is inexorably linked with goal-directed activity, and both of these with the underlying mental stability that we call sanity. The loss of self-definition therefore precipitates a crisis in which the world and the self alternately become "unreal." I am not speaking here merely of Romantic alienation, but

Vision of the Voyage

of a frightening recognition of emptiness which the Romantic alien may occasionally experience.

This recognition of emptiness is the subject of "Paraphrase," which pictures a mind able to grasp only the spaces between its own thoughts. We are reminded again of Coleridge, who was interested in the "Nightmare Life-in-Death" as a symbol of the horrible mental state which has lost its former categorical definition but which cannot adopt a new one. Carlyle also presented this dilemma in the "Centre of Indifference." In Crane, though, the experience is more terrifying than in Coleridge or Carlyle, because even the momentarily submerged faith in the mind to be reborn, to put on new clothes, is absent here. "Paraphrase" is thus a poem about panic and despair.

The inversion of the long sentence composing the first stanza diffuses our sense of individual consciousness.

> Of a steady winking beat between
> Systole, diastole spokes-of-a-wheel
> One rushing from the bed at night
> May find the record wedged in his soul.

The subject òf the sentence, "One," seems to be lost among the other elements. Then the person's body becomes increasingly depersonalized by repeated use of the article "the," until the last stanza when "your" suddenly appears. Throughout, the experience is fragmented and uninterpreted; no explanation is suggested as to what is happening or to whom. We find in the first stanza that detachment from the self so familiar now in Crane's poetry. One may come with a start, it says, to sense within oneself the emptiness and silence which constantly fall between heart beats; they are the death we carry with us.

But it is as if the person "rushing from the bed" had somehow left his own body. For the second stanza finds the body still beneath the sheets. This stanza and the next two represent various parts of the body unresponsive to any external stimuli. The space between the beats, like the land of "North Labrador," never

White Buildings: *The Character of Crane's Lyric*

knows change. There is no interplay between mind and world; the nearest comparison to this state of unknowing is staring without seeing at the white space between roses on the wallpaper.

The confrontation with despair, Crane's *saison en enfer,* will play an important part in *The Bridge*. It is a crucial fact in Romantic psychology. The willingness to examine and record even the most dreaded emotional experience is the trial by fire of the Romantic. And the most dreaded experience is the point at which the illusion of well-being drops away and one must face the breakdown of his world into chaos. Grasping and accepting the inevitability of his own destruction is the most difficult phase in the education of a Romantic. It replaces any mythology his culture gives him, insisting on the ultimate triumph of phenomena over all categorical knowledge. In this way his agonizing descent toward nothingness insures his commitment to noncommitment as a critic of culture; it gives to gratifying emotions, when they return, a beauty and power greater than any they possessed before; and it imparts to his whole intellectual endeavor the saving grace of humility.

If there is no foundation for identity, nothing lasting and "real" that we know as ourselves, what is it we contemplate in introspection? The answer must be our past configurations of knowledge, our memories of the styles of behavior (especially perception) which have thus far constituted reality for us. One of the most important of these styles is our habitual way of responding to our own behavior, insistently construing it as consistent and of a piece. This is the illusion of identity. Wordsworth, in the *Prelude* and in "Tintern Abbey," probed the sense of identity, first, by turning from society and its roles which stabilize those habits of behavior and, second, by examining himself in the repetition of an experience, such as visiting a place he had loved as a boy. Crane does the same thing in "Repose of Rivers."

Crane has returned to the Isle of Pines and is recalling what he had forgotten for so long, what the sounds and feelings there meant to him as a boy. These memories are revived in a highly

Vision of the Voyage

stylized form. The sound of wind through the trees is described as a sarabande, and heavy alliteration contributes to the musical effect. In the second stanza weeds become flags, and the alcoves, cypresses, and turtles are remembered in a kind of dream sequence and are imbued now with great value. These memories in their simplified and intensified form are preferred to the more immediate memories of the city which become equally stylized, but nightmarishly so. Such mental distortion is unavoidable, for all things "nurse" memory. The hurricane winds of the recent visit are even superimposed on the earlier memory of the steady sound through the willows. But Crane's present experience refuses to be confined by memory or stylization. The brilliant metaphor, "wind flaking sapphire," seems to break down the boundaries of comprehension. This metaphor illustrates Crane's ability to sustain a tension between the phenomenal world and the constructs for interpreting it. Our mind lags behind this image as we try to comprehend it. Crane is demonstrating the fact that phenomenal reality challenges the mind to conceive it in each new moment of apprehension. "Repose of Rivers" charts the process of introspection beginning with memory, in which reality and identity seem so objective and manageable that the luxury of preference can be entertained, and ending with immediate fact, which is either thrilling or terrifying, but always uncompromising in its demands.

The triumph of fact over conceptualization is also the central theme of "Emblems of Conduct," Crane's fascinating pastiche of fragments from Samuel Greenberg. The apostle, the orators, and the historians represent those roles played by an individual when he tries to objectify and codify certain experiences of great value. Such experiences are represented in the poem by the power and beauty of the volcano, by joy—the most affirmative emotion—, by the universe followed by the orators, and by the past with its heroes. As soon as the response of affirmation is objectified in the erupting volcano it begins to degenerate into a limited conceptualization. People are "lured" into spiritual gates

White Buildings: *The Character of Crane's Lyric*

when they assign a certain "meaning" to an experience of great value. For their next step is to try to deduce other behavior from that conceptualized meaning. The "complete laws" and "discipline" which institutions enforce pretend to derive from and be justified by a "spiritual" reality. This deduction amounts to constructing a constitutive metaphysic, which drains away the life-giving tension between experience and our understanding of it.

The wanderer, however, is the Romantic, who is neither an apostle nor one of the people. He is depicted here as a painter, like Bill Sommer in "Sunday Morning Apples," for he experiments with interpretational models of the world. Notice in the last stanza, when the wanderer's position is presented, how the perspective suddenly shifts. Clouds stretching into the horizon are seen as supporting the sea. And the archs of the swimming dolphins, like the boy running before the sun in Brandywine, change the shape of reality for the artist. Unlike the official interpreters of reality, he appreciates the importance of spiritual gates (the symbolization of the sense of value) without idolizing them. He understands that objective realities (including spiritual ones) are like summer and smoke, short-lived and forever changing shape. In this way he remains free from the commitment his society would impose on him; it does not matter to him who the chosen hero is or what his program might be. For the wanderer's mind is categorically as fluid as reality is unpredictable. He has defeated what Nietzsche called the "will to truth."[15]

Defeating the "will to truth," pursuing Crane's "bright logic," amounts to rejecting interpretations of experience which function as false masks. These are explanations which preserve current patterns of behavior by diverting attention from the interests at work in them. The Romantic, I suggested, is continually approaching Hegelian absolute knowledge. That is, he subjects his experience to a kind of investigation which brings it to the

[15]*Beyond Good and Evil,* trans. Kaufmann, p. 9.

point of changing; in this way he frees his reality from the determining forces of his society and from those of his own personality. We have seen some of the hazards of this intellectual endeavor in "Paraphrase" and "Chaplinesque." But another difficulty—for Crane and for the reader—is apparent in "Possessions."

How does the Romantic conceptualize his experience without the categories of value in his culture? The creation of a unique style for the apprehension of reality and the extension of the meaningful meaningless have been solutions to this problem, as we have seen. But in "Possessions" and several more of the longer lyrics in *White Buildings* we appreciate how challenging the experimentation with metaphor can become. The difficulty of this poem lies chiefly in the way Crane delays interpretational clues which serve gradually to orient the reader.

> Witness now this trust! the rain
> That steals softly direction
> And the key, ready to hand—sifting
> One moment in sacrifice (the direst)
> Through a thousand nights the flesh
> Assaults outright for bolts that linger
> Hidden,—O undirected as the sky
> That through its black foam has no eyes
> For this fixed stone of lust . . .

"Trust," "rain," and "key" in the first stanza are like elements in a mysterious allegory that seem to need interpretation by the last word "lust." The induction of confusion or the temporary suspension of interpretation is an important stylistic innovation of Romanticism. It serves to isolate the issues in the poem from contexts in which we ordinarily consider them. If we think the poem is somehow about "lust" but are uncertain what our response to this word should be after that puzzling first stanza, we are not likely to fall back on the comfortable responses appropriate in other contexts. Instead we labor to give images of

White Buildings: *The Character of Crane's Lyric*

the poem new meanings relevant to whatever interpretational clues are available. Placing a category of value in a relatively bizzare context so that its conventional meaning is no longer appropriate is a modern poetic technique of Romantic origins.

"Possessions," like "Chaplinesque," suggests a strategy for coping with an almost unbearable situation, and also like "Chaplinesque" it ends with a change in the way reality is apprehended. The feelings presented early in the poem, resulting from cycles of obsessive lust, are experienced passively as oppressive. But they are not rejected, conceived as undesirable, or avoided. Rather, these painful feelings, examples of "the states of passion, experience and rumination that fate forces on the poet first hand," which Crane talked about in "General Aims and Theories," are acknowledged and focused upon sharply. In this way the passive attitude of oppression is replaced by the active one of acceptance, and the character of the feelings changes. What was torment turns in the last two lines to great emotional relief. The point to grasp is that organized responses consistently elicited by given signs (sexual ones, for example, of whatever type), will continue to exert their influence over an individual as long as he relates to them as knower to known, conceptualizing the signs and their meanings as part of the "external world." The stimulus-response distinction is one of the most effective false masks, which tends always to stabilize whatever feelings the individual identifies in himself. This poem presents the transformation of those feelings by penetrating that false mask. The individual experiences tremendous pressure from society and from his own personality to accept value definitions for his behavior. Whether he obeys the definitions or evades them matters little in his submission to the urge toward "personal integrity." The Romantic alternative spoken for here is accepting and exploring emotions which are severely policed by cultural definition. Sustaining insouciance toward those definitions eventually frees the individual from the tortuous emotional devices of social and personal management.

Vision of the Voyage

The "possessions," then, are feelings which the poet discovers in himself. And the "trust" of the first line refers to a confidence in the individual's power to endure both a reality which is painful and the state of mind characterized by less and less definition which must precede a restructuring of experience. It also refers to the confidence extended to the reader in this poem, which is a personal confession about sexual desire. The rain and the black clouds which cover everything suggest the oppressiveness of obsessive sexual interests. And the key is the acquiescence to and pursuit of these fascinations. The point of decision to seek again the same thrill which has captivated or "possessed" the poet countless times before is an exhilarating and reckless moment. Its intensity and sameness, its unqualified tyranny over the poet are symbolized by the "fixed stone."

The second stanza begins to assess the value of all the poet's sexual adventures. They are worth, first, the experience of sex itself, which is sovereign in its power and, in a sense, always the same. The last four lines of this stanza express the anticipation, excitement, and fulfillment of orgasm with its aftercalm. Then in the third stanza the poet reconsiders sex, not as a pure and isolated experience of great value, but in the context of his whole life. He "takes up" the knowledge of his lust, as one would a burden, assuming it as quietly as desire "stole" upon him at the beginning of the first stanza. He is caustically self-conscious in the underground world where he seeks gratification. But he does not merely regret his situation; he confronts it as directly as possible. Like an animal roasting on a spit, he sees himself trapped and tortured by his own emotions.

Exhausted by these feelings, he retains of the wasteful and frustrating memories only his willingness to face and record them. This, however, precipitates what he calls the "pure possession." Earlier, sexual feelings and agonies associated with them were called "possessions," and Crane had been, in a sense, "possessed" by these feelings. In contrast, this possession is "pure"; it is compared to fire and a hurricane wind. And it

White Buildings: *The Character of Crane's Lyric*

changes the poet's attitude toward his sexual disposition. The oppressive, immobile "fixed stone of lust" has become "bright stones wherein our smiling plays." Let me suggest that by "pure possession" Crane means experience, here sexual experience, under the aspect of absolute knowledge. Actual sexual experience takes place, of course, in the brutal world of cultural definition. There the poet's feelings toward sex must alternate between clandestine thrills in which he ignores everything but erotic qualities, and depression in which those qualities lose their value and he sees them in their societal contexts. In other words the interpretation of sexual experience, especially for the deviant, can easily lead to self-degradation and self-pity if the value definitions of society which police behavior have been incorporated into his personality: he can become his own judge and executioner. "Possessions" explores this self-victimization and asserts an alternative to it. Although there is no real escape from the situation, the individual can pursue a kind of interpretation of experience whose end is not the policing of behavior. For Crane this meant writing poetry about that experience. In this way value (both the positive value of erotic fascination and the negative value of regret) is transferred for a time from the dangerous and exhausting world of social realities to the work of art. Striving to understand and represent experience in all its painful contradictions and absurdities replaces the deluding goals of personal fulfillment, normality or rebellion, and integrity. The images of destruction in the last lines suggest the purging of experience, and the images of light echo Crane's earlier association of lucidity with the disintegration of categorical knowledge which defines social roles.

We have already seen some of the implications of this understanding of categorical knowledge for personal identity. "Recitative" further explores the puzzle of what one really considers in introspection. It posits a situation in which the poet looks into a hand mirror and addresses his own image. Each stanza elaborates and qualifies the relationship between the speaker and what he

White Buildings: *The Character of Crane's Lyric*

attempts to identify as "himself." The first two stanzas emphasize the paradoxical nature of this relationship. For although the poet and his image are "the same," they are also irreconcilably different. Like the two faces of Janus which never see each other, they remain mysterious to each other. Just as the eyes of the reflection cannot comprehend the meaning of the poet's face, neither can the poet understand himself by looking in a mirror. For his response to his own image, like his response to any sign configuration, is determined by interests immediately inaccessible to him. His style of apprehending himself has been shaped over the years by the problems which have made up his mental life. Now, however, he tries to see himself purely, without any ulterior motives. And the results are frustrating. In the third stanza a smile becomes a challenge for the poet to interpret. For he must resist the conventionalized responses which have thus far defined that gesture and at the same time avoid losing the ability to respond with genuine emotion. Then in the fourth stanza he turns to experience, which has no more substance than his identity. It is first fragmented and chaotic, then harmonious.

But the objectivity with which the poet stands back, as it were, and views himself and his own experience does not allow him finally to "know himself" or to determine that experience. The fifth stanza suggests that the poet in introspection is like a man standing on the top of a tall building or like Absalom suspended by his hair about to be killed. He is aware of all the choices made by him and for him that have given his world its meaning and shape. And he cannot begin again; it is always too late for that. But the desire to reshape one's life, to be somehow what one should have been is itself a false mask. It results in the kind of self-pity we saw combatted in "Possessions" which only adds pain to an already stabilized pattern of behavior. The last two stanzas point to an alternative attitude toward experience and one's self. Although it is true that one's habits of perception are irrevocably created and reinforced in time and that self-definition is as necessary as it is limiting, it is also true that the past in

Vision of the Voyage

which those habits were formed and the self-definitions made is irretrievably lost. As we have seen, that past is "real" only to the extent that it is interpreted, and the mind's sovereign prerogative is to mediate knowledge, change its interpretation of reality. The present, therefore, is always indeterminate. And since all knowledge is metaphoric, one may as easily construe himself on a bridge as on top of a tower. Crane, then, associates the tower (his own accumulated victimizing interests) with society, which is as corrupt as Nineveh, and dissociates himself from it. While his will (the prerogative to respond inappropriately to any situation, even one long associated with himself) claims the bridge for its new symbol. The last stanza draws on an important Romantic idea, the synopsis of eternity into a single moment.

> In alternating bells have you not heard
> All hours clapped dense into a single stride?

These lines express a realization of the mind's power to dissociate itself from cultural definitions, to free itself from its own and society's interests, so that the meaning of reality may change and become virtually anything. The feeling of eternity is the sense of freedom from circumstantial limitation.

At the end of the poem Crane is fully aware of his contradictory attitudes toward himself: on the one hand as a pseudoentity realized only in action and knowable only in culturally defined terms, and on the other hand as absolute freedom and as an undifferentiated process of becoming. In the last two lines Crane even apologizes for speaking at such length about what everyone must already know in order to get out of bed in the morning. To accept exclusively one view of the self or the other would be to yield to euphoria or despair; Crane accepts both views, sustaining the irreconcilable tension between them.

This poem, and all the others we have examined in *White Buildings,* come out of an introspection possible only in a state of cultural alienation. Although in some of them other individuals are present, it is the poet's own changing apprehension of these

Vision of the Voyage

individuals that interests us. Crane never forgets that knowledge of other people, like any knowledge, is the result of categorical mediation and that interests are always assumed to lie behind that knowledge. In other words one knows and relates to other individuals on the basis of motives which are defined and policed by one's culture. Therefore to know a person is always, in a sense, to use that person. But the Romantic alien is in the awkward position of knowing people and knowing how he knows them. Rather than focusing upon the false masks of human relationships (those interests which justify and stabilize them), he focuses instead on ulterior interests which, when grasped, threaten the relationships with dissolution. Sustaining alienation while examining nonalienated individuals as they use each other and victimize themselves is the subject of one of Crane's most powerful poems, "The Wine Menagerie."

This poem is set in a speakeasy as the poet sits at the bar drinking and watching a man and a woman having an argument. The first two stanzas introduce some of the poet's mental experiments which will explain how he is observing that argument. These experiments reveal his ability to control apprehension of the scene through a highly selective style of perception.

> Invariably when wine redeems the sight,
> Narrowing the mustard scansions of the eyes,
> A leopard ranging always in the brow
> Asserts a vision in the slumbering gaze.
>
> Then glozening decanters that reflect the street
> Wear me in crescents on their bellies. Slow
> Applause flows into liquid cynosures:
> —I am conscripted to their shadows' glow.

Alcohol helps to cultivate such a style, and the poet begins to see himself and those around him with aesthetic detachment, as if he found himself in a menagerie. His eyes seem to change their shape and way of seeing, the pupils narrowing like the mustard-colored eyes of a leopard. And his own shape is redefined by the

White Buildings: *The Character of Crane's Lyric*

bottles that reflect his image while he makes no attempt to remember how he "really" looks sober. He surrenders entirely to his intoxication, indulging whatever associations come to mind. The sound of wine poured into a glass is like slow applause filling an auditorium.

Then in the third stanza the poet turns and looks at the couple sitting against the dirty black wainscoting. The list that begins "snow, eggs, yarn . . ." suggests the heavy reliance on metaphor that is determining how the poet sees the scene and isolating his interpretation from anyone else's in the bar. What he sees in the faces of the couple is an uncompromising struggle for mastery. The man's smile is a possessive instrument. So are the woman's eyes, seeing the situation with her own designs, viciously ironic to the man's. He is furious, sweat popping out on his throbbing temples; she is unyielding, cruel. The will in both cases is personified by the serpent, which, like the leopard in the poet's brow, is associated with the eyes in order to suggest a cunning, preying quality in the purposefulness of seeing. Each look considers itself holy and precious, justifying its own murderous intentions with elegance and beauty.

The entrance of the urchin in stanza five heightens our sense of the separateness in which each individual lives. Like the poet, he is not really a part of the world of the speakeasy. Crane sees him as a visitor from the snow who really belongs to the summer out of doors. But he only briefly interrupts the battle of wills which resumes in even more horrible guise in stanza six. The lines of the couple's faces and bodies are abstracted and express in themselves the ruthless character of the exchanges. Every defense is countered with another new accusation. Notice, also, though, that the beauty of the struggle is emphasized: "Between black tusks the roses shine!" Crane is stylizing the encounter, demonstrating how the same situation can be an occasion for vastly different responses on his part. He sees the motivations and strategies of mutual exploitation in the figures before him,

Vision of the Voyage

but he does not identify with these motives. And he can just as easily focus upon the scene with only his aesthetic interests.

Stanza seven makes just this point very forcefully. It is Crane's formulation of what Keats called "negative capability," the ability to suspend one's habitual patterns of response, which are goal-oriented, in order to structure a new pattern on the model of another person or thing.

> New thresholds, new anatomies! Wine talons
> Build freedom up about me and distill
> This competence—to travel in a tear
> Sparkling alone, within another's will.

It is not important whether or not the poet really feels exactly the way someone else does. He could never know if he did or not. The point to grasp is that the culturally defined needs and desires which determine how the poet experiences reality temporarily lose their power over him. He uses another person, or even an animal or an object, as a stylistic principle for the selection and organization of his responses into a pattern that he has thus far identified as an other. In this way he frees himself temporarily from his own social roles, and sensing this freedom he is fortified.

But we must be sure to understand how this poem, like the previous one, goes beyond transcendentalism. Crane does not merely celebrate cultural transcendence and the redemptive hopes it engenders. He is also willing to question the psychological strategy of alienation, to dissociate himself even from cultural transcendence in order to understand its limitations. In stanza eight he describes how he sustains alienation by modeling his responses on stylistic principles taken first from one person's behavior, then from another's. With the proper attitude of reception he continues "snaring the purities" of other people's feelings and actions. Then he goes on to point out the context from which

White Buildings: *The Character of Crane's Lyric*

these behavior patterns come, and we see how his use of them differs from that original context. As he adopts each new pattern as a temporary identity, he recognizes it as a shell—a shell of sound chimed by those in hell—around his disinterested self, a "flame of gaunt repose." The hell referred to is the hell of living, very much like Sartre's, in which each man must accept the limitations imposed on his own being by the choices he makes, choices invariably involving the exploitation of others and of himself.

Every style of behavior is originally a strategy of mastery in some problem situation, but the poet has his own uniquely Romantic interests in these styles. He does not accept the limitations they would impose on him; they are only masks ("dominoes" in the ninth stanza) which he takes up one after another and lays down.

The last three stanzas describe the psychological dilemma in which the poet has involved himself, beginning with the paradoxical conception of his skill as "frozen billows." No matter how successful he is as an emotional chameleon or as a poet, the fundamental psychological problem he has discovered is inescapable. Self-definition or role playing, although it may amount to wearing masks, is all one really can do. Loving and hating create the only world there is, so eluding victimization and exploitation may give the poet freedom and even insure him fame (the sand suggests an hour glass), but the resulting alienation also gives him pain. He knows, then, that he has victimized himself, in a sense, by his own Romantic strategy.

But once he has grasped certain insights and let his life be shaped around them, that alienation is unavoidable. The "tooth implicit of the world" expresses the profound pessimism to which Romanticism and Crane are committed. The last two stanzas present the poet walking away from all he has seen and felt in the bar, epitomized in the decapitated Holofernes and John the Baptist. The destruction of men by women, especially as in Petrushka's case in return for love, is a pathetic dramatization of

Vision of the Voyage

the basic dilemma on which society must stand: interaction is a process of limiting behavior, possible only through the defeat of certain interests and the concealment of others. Viciousness and deception, then, are inescapable psychological conditions. But to accept alienation, as Crane does in this poem, is to understand these conditions in a supramoral sense. That is, they are not evils to be redeemed or avoided; indeed they cannot be avoided. Actually they are interests too powerful and dangerous to remain masked by morality. Thus the poet is willing to see them in others and in himself in order to place all behavior, including his own, under the most rigorous scrutiny. Conceiving a ruthless self-interest to lie at the heart of all behavior, as Nietzsche did in his "will to power," brings into serious question those existing explanations which rely on morality. In "The Wine Menagerie" Crane sees a force similar to Nietzsche's at work in the scene before him and thus is able to dissociate himself from malicious social interests, although he is not able to free himself from the mind's continuing domination of the world it discovers.

If we bear this point in mind, that the Romantic cannot escape the mental processes he is examining, the self-critical character of the poems in *White Buildings* is understandable. The poet must become, as it were, an other to himself in order to comprehend his experience without the interests which he ordinarily takes for granted. This is the reason for the internal dialogues and the various other techniques Crane uses to achieve a detachment from his own feelings. One cannot, that is to say, decide to know oneself with Socratic composure. On the contrary, approaching self-knowledge for the Romantic has always meant placing himself in the dangerous and almost intolerable position in which his emotional reactions serve no conventional purpose. As a result, he cannot identify any role as "himself." He knows that no propositional knowledge is permanently useful in identifying the self. Paradoxically, self-knowledge for the Romantic must be a process of resisting self-definition. This is the process Crane examines in "Passage."

White Buildings: *The Character of Crane's Lyric*

One resists self-definition by forcing himself repeatedly to confront the phenomenal world, that is, to allow current mediating constructs to be destroyed and new ones formed. This process is not begun, however, without its own justifying mask. The hope that leads the poet forward is transcendentalist redemption, expressed in the first stanza as "an improved infancy." The desire to recover a Wordsworthian purer self or to achieve some sort of self-realization lies behind the poet's dangerous quest. It is a quest which begins in the discovery of the potential fluidity of categorical distinctions making alienation possible. Notice that the sound of the sea is associated with the categorical realignment which occurs in the first line, when the cedar leaf seems to divide the sky. The sea often represents for Crane the eternally shifting, yet also eternally identical, phenomenal world, which ultimately resists or destroys all man's attempts to conceptualize it. But here it is enough to say that Crane introduces the sea to suggest the absolute freedom and the mystery which underlie all responses. The realization of this freedom is the foundation of transcendentalist redemption with which the poem begins.

So the poet continues the process of alienation, as we have seen he must, by dissociating himself from the fictionalizing process of memory. In the second stanza Crane characterizes this faculty as parasitic and deluding. It must be left behind because it generalizes by obscuring differences and combines by associations. Crane is consistent in his use of light imagery; memory is here associated with darkness and the moon, which can make the shadow apron of a rock seem substantial. It becomes a bum in a dark alley.

But as he continues, the original promise is not fulfilled. The wind which had symbolized his freedom dies, and the burning sun which had augured the defeat of memory gives place to chimney soot and heavy smoke returning on itself. The poet has learned a lesson from transcendentalism or from trying to be a transcendentalist. The hope that alienation will perfect the

Vision of the Voyage

individual, that it will be a solution rather than a new set of problems, is abortive. In fact, striving to become something through alienation is self-defeating; one can only lose the sense of being something. In the last three stanzas the poet discovers that the "improved infancy," actually a state of mind possible only through a highly selective application of memory, is a mask that must be penetrated.

This penetration occurs in an internal dialogue remarkably like the dream sequence in the *Prelude*, Book Five. In Wordsworth's poem the dreamer meets a figure riding a camel in the desert; he is both an Arab and Don Quixote, holding a stone (mathematical science) in one hand and a beautiful shell (poetry) in the other. From the shell the dreamer hears an ode foretelling the destruction of the world by a flood, and the figure hurries away to bury these objects—now called books—as the waters chase after him. Note particularly that the overwhelming flood is described as "a bed of glittering light," and compare Crane's "Sand troughed us in a glittering abyss." Wordsworth is saying that the creative genius of man is strangely incompatible with the mutable elements which he must use to embody his visions. The end of the parable suggests that all man's endeavors must eventually be lost because of the nature of the world in which they are realized. Crane would not disagree.

But whereas Wordsworth's poem only suggests the paradoxical position man finds himself in, Crane's "Passage" goes on to refute the very tendency to hope for permanence. His narrator "argues with the laurel" and plays the wily sprite before memory and all conceptualization, represented by the thief with the stolen book. Withstanding the temptation to accept a formulation of reality as final requires the grimmest irony. Smiling in the irrefutable face of death is not putting it too strongly. Now in the last stanza the poet, freed from memory and from any hope of deliverance from problems, can actually confront the phenomenal world. What does he see?

White Buildings: *The Character of Crane's Lyric*

>He closed the book. And from the Ptolemies
>Sand troughed us in a glittering abyss.
>A serpent swam a vertex to the sun
>—On unpaced beaches leaned its tongue and
>   drummed.
>What fountains did I hear? what icy speeches?
>Memory, committed to the page, had broke.

There cannot be an answer. The last stanza of the poem, which reminds us strongly of Coleridge's "Kubla Khan," must end with an undetermined vision and mystery. For the point is that only fictions and a victimizing memory can provide the basis for interpreting experience. One approaches absolute knowledge only to find that there is nothing to be said about reality. When all man's systematic knowledge from the time of Ptolemy to the present is temporarily lost in the chaos of phenomena, the poet can only ask "meaningless" questions until he returns to old fictions or makes new ones. Therefore "Passage" might as well be titled "Becoming," for it is about the unidentifiable process we must continually conceptualize and thus falsify. The poem may also be said to dramatize the process leading to cultural innovation, whereby freedom from preconceptions and expectancies allows new patterns of behavior to come into being.

The longer poems of *White Buildings* have in common a certain attitude which is consistently celebrated. It is a willingness to dissociate oneself from interests in problem situations, especially those interests which are extremely attractive and dangerous. This amounts to a disavowal of anything which promises to be a solution; one's allegiance, or tendency to identify with specific value formulations, is suspended. For example, Crane's own sexual fascinations in "Possessions" and his desire for certainty and peace in "Passage" are not finally what the poet focuses upon. No, our real interest in these two poems centers in Crane's own examination and analysis of the values with which he is involved. I have tried to demonstrate

Vision of the Voyage

that, similarly, much of our interest in Crane's imagery centers in his calling attention to the stylistic principles on which the imagery is organized. We might say that Crane's poems make experience self-conscious. They dramatize the fact that highly charged emotions and our habits of perception, which determine the shape and quality of life, endure only through self-deception. This necessary condition of self-deception may be discussed in a number of ways; I have chosen to call it a belief in the *reality* of the self and of the external world. Crane strives in his poetry to dissolve the objectivity of experience, its thing-quality, by assuming a relentlessly self-critical attitude toward his own perceptions and feelings. His application of metaphor, his aesthetic perspective, and his disinterested first-person technique present experience as an organization of responses; discovering and presenting a believable principle for that organization threatens the stability of the experience, bringing it to the point of change. But Crane not only demonstrates this self-critical attitude toward experience, he celebrates it. What is important in a problem situation is not its outcome but one's success in relating to it with Romantic irony. The celebration of this special kind of control over one's experience is the subject of "Lachrymae Christi."

The title refers ambiguously to an object of meditation, the tears of Christ, as well as to a Neapolitan wine. The whole poem depends upon this ambiguity, which is dramatized at the end when Christ becomes, for the poet, Dionysus. Also the earlier description of the factory scene by moonlight exploits, in ways we have noticed before, the ambiguity of perception. Every object in that scene is metaphorically transfigured; nothing in the least conventional remains of the factory windows reflecting the moonlight or of the stream reflecting the machinery. Indeed the directives we are given, so to speak, for imagining the landscape force us to exercise to the fullest our unappreciated prerogative to reconstrue any configuration on the basis of a new stylistic model.

White Buildings: *The Character of Crane's Lyric*

>Whitely, while benzine
>Rinsings from the moon
>Dissolve all but the windows of the mills
>(Inside the sure machinery
>Is still
>And curdled only where a sill
>Sluices its one unyielding smile)

We see only the windows of the mill, because the moon has dissolved everything else into darkness, just as benzine might act on cloth as a solvent in the mill. And inside, the metal is reflected in the water and distorted (curdled) as it is seen in the arch of splashes over the sluice. The "fox's teeth" might refer to the teeth of gears, also inside, but since the rest of the stanza takes place outside the mill, this image should probably be taken literally. The whiteness of the moon seems to color those clean deadly teeth, as thorns on the hill are coated red with the blood of animals which have brushed by them. Our interest in the landscape and the factory lies chiefly in new possibilities Crane offers for perceiving them. But it is not enough to say that Crane has given us a very unusual picture of a scene by moonlight. He has given us both an artificial and a natural landscape to which we respond in the first two stanzas entirely with aesthetic interest. That is to say, our principles for selecting and organizing the sensory data serve to suspend our interpretation of the scene itself. Crane presents the scene like a painting whose arrangement of space and color interest us more than its recognizable subject. Although the subject may hold strong emotional biases for us, these biases are temporarily forgotten while we concentrate on the stylistic principles at work. So in this poem the dense and foreign metaphors create a stylistic abstraction on which the mind quite actively plays, experiments.

No first person reference has yet appeared, but these two stanzas present the landscape from a distinctively personal point of view, which will be identified as the speaker's in stanza six.

Vision of the Voyage

Now, though, the poet's mind continues to transform the scene before him. Nature, which is characterized in stanza two as dangerous and indifferent under the verbal arabesque, is now purified in stanza three. The moonlight and darkness of night have "opened" a whole new world unbound by time. The imagination is free to compose reality into any order which might redeem it.

> And the nights opening
> Chant pyramids,—
> Anoint with innocence,—recall
> To music and retrieve what perjuries
> Had galvanized the eyes.

Such a night could easily contain pyramids or yield a fantastic visual music. But we are aware in this third stanza that such a redemption is only a triumph of the imagination. Here is an example of that application of metaphor which sustains rather than conceals the discrepancy between the world and our conceptualization of it. And it is most important to bear in mind that redemption is a matter of enforced style when we come to the figure of Christ in stanza five: "Thy Nazarene and tinder eyes." The hymn to Christ, who becomes Dionysus, begins as a hymn to all life, for every object and sound is interpreted as a sign of blessing and joy. Even the imagined sound of worms in the earth, or of underground trains serving the mills, sing unqualified praises to life. And regret, here as in "Legend," has no place. "Penitence" always serves to solidify an old formulation of the world, and this poem is concerned with the mind's prerogative of absolute freedom in the interpretation of reality. The two poems thus complement each other in their attitudes toward regret.

The inversion of the long sentence comprising the fourth and fifth stanzas ("While chime/Beneath . . . ") places special emphasis on the pun, "tinder." Like the word play of the title, this pun calls attention to the potential ambiguity in experience. A

White Buildings: *The Character of Crane's Lyric*

painting of Christ can easily be imagined which portrays tender, submissive eyes, but substituting "tinder" in the last line gives the reader the experience of actually seeing the character of those eyes change. They become intensely aggressive, perhaps even erotic. And the eyes of Christ are a profound and far-reaching symbol; they suggest a point of view which is absolutely beyond question and which is capable of enduring any amount of persecution. They extend to the religious beholder the responsibility for continual self-examination and repentance. But here it is clear that the meaning of those eyes is, after all, a function of the beholder's willingness to see them in an appropriate way. Changing one letter in the fifth stanza effects a metamorphosis. So this ambiguous religious object is shown to be subject to the same stylistic determination as the earlier moonlit scene. The poem demonstrates that the mind has, in effect, discovered its own freedom. And in the next stanza we understand how this discovery takes place.

> (Let sphinxes from the ripe
> Borage of death have cleared my tongue
> Once and again; vermin and rod
> No longer bind. Some sentient cloud
> Of tears flocks through the tendoned loam:
> Betrayed stones slowly speak.)

The realization of death has freed the poet from the needs satisfied by those languishing eyes. He begins to see Christ in a new way. It is as if his vision of the ultimate and irremediable loss of all things and of himself had grown gradually like a plant (borage) and finally yielded a cordial that, when drunk, freed his mind and tongue from old bonds. This new knowledge is expressed as liberated sphinxes. That is, paradoxes and unanswerable questions no longer intimidate the poet, forcing him to create solutions or answers by denying certain aspects of his experience. The program of repentance, in other words, characterized by the monastic "vermin and rod" is now rejected. The sentence "Some sentient cloud/Of tears flocks through the ten-

Vision of the Voyage

doned loam" fuses images of earth and body. "Flocks" probably alludes to the animals on the hill whose hides were pricked by the thorns. A regeneration of feeling occurs in the poet just as easily as that flock, perhaps of sheep (seen as one mass, like a cloud), moves across the land. The "tendoned loam" is the poet's own body, so the "betrayed stones" are parts of himself, aspects of his experience which had been suppressed or unacknowledged. The sheep on the hill, then, since they participate in the destructive aspects of nature, which only man calls cruel, symbolize the poet's new acceptance of suffering and oblivion. This stanza suggests that the desire for special sanctuary is itself abortive, deriving from the need for protection, not from phenomenal reality, but from the inadequacies of our conceptualizations of it. From the mind's attempts to understand the world come notions of very limited usefulness, whose consequences, as they are logically pursued, terrify us. Our own metaphors lead us to panic.

The "names" we give experience, especially in the pursuit of resolution, are the only real cruelty in the world. These are exemplified in stanza seven ("Names peeling from Thine eyes") by the ecclesiastical year, itself centering around the crucifixion. But the next stanza prepares for the transformation of Christ into Dionysus. Notice that this eighth stanza ("Lean long from sable, slender boughs") is in the imperative mood. The poet accepts the prerogative to reinterpret the symbol of the crucifix. The cross becomes a graceful slender tree. And the nights, which before had represented redemption purely as a stylistic ordering of experience, place the mythical figure in a new focus. They generate around him concentric circles, so that his face seems to fall in the center of a target. The grail, like the one at the conclusion of "Chaplinesque," represents experience which is highly valued simply by virtue of the mind's fiat; the grail is associated with earth, not with heaven or the sacraments. The image of lilac-emerald breath appropriately brings together the ideas both of spring or regeneration and of death. That face

White Buildings: *The Character of Crane's Lyric*

which, as it lifts, is recognized to be the face of Dionysus must rise "From charred and riven stakes" and not from some pleasing stylization, because this god actually symbolizes that destructive aspect of becoming which a sentimentalization of Christ would defeat.

The best commentary on Dionysus in this poem is *The Birth of Tragedy,* which Crane knew at least indirectly.[16] In that work Nietzsche emphasizes the degeneracy of the whole intellectual tradition deriving from Socrates. That tradition, he says, is founded on a falsehood: that we can know the world and effect beneficial changes within it. And, on this assumption, tradition constructs a morality with absolute standards, as it relegates art to the realm of delusion and lies. However the only real lie, Nietzsche would say, is the optimism on which this tradition rests. And continuing the assault upon that optimism, an assault begun by Kant in the sphere of logic and carried on by the Romantics, Nietzsche proposes that we embrace the pessimism which he saw at the heart of Greek tragedy. The world is redeemed, he says, only by illusion: "only as an aesthetic phenomenon is existence and the world eternally justified."[17] The drive to penetrate illusion, to accept the oblivion toward which we move, and at the same time to celebrate life as beautiful and pleasurable he calls Dionysian. Dionysus is associated with intoxication (as opposed to Apollonian dreams) and with music, and he carries us through intense suffering to joy.

Now Crane's poem makes considerable sense in just these terms. One breaks through illusion, first of all, by grasping the potential ambiguity of all experience. As we have seen, Crane

---

[16]See Crane's essay "The Case Against Nietzsche" in *The Complete Poems,* pp. 197-198, and Brom Weber's discussion of Nietzsche's influence on Crane in *Hart Crane, A Biographical and Critical Study* (New York: Bodley Press, 1948), pp. 18-22.

[17]*The Birth of Tragedy,* trans. Walter Kaufmann (New York: Random House, 1967), p. 52.

forces the reader to grasp that ambiguity through the poem's self-consciously metaphorical descriptions. And the metamorphosis of Christ into Dionysus is really a disavowal of parochial and puritanical allegiances. Christ's suffering yields tears which are also wine. The deepest suffering need not, in other words, nurture a complacent broken spirit. It may lead to an acceptance of what to the fear-ridden rational mind is unacceptable and thus unlock the heart to joy. The acceptance, or more properly the transcendence, of pessimism frees the individual from the need of protection and deliverance which guilt nurtures. The only possible evasion of the destructiveness and loss which characterize reality in becoming is illusion—specifically the belief in the enduring subsistence of individual objects through time. But Crane demonstrates that objectivity, thing-ness, is a discipline of the mind, and a dangerous discipline, for it seduces with an unfounded optimism. Breaking down the categorical boundaries of experience (stripping away false masks) frees the mind from its illusions. This has its own dangers, but it restores to the individual his vital sense of spontaneity and of beauty. His life takes on the wholeness and rightness of no longer requiring apology or justification.

These statements apply as well to Crane's most Nietzchean poem, "For the Marriage of Faustus and Helen." In fact, if we bear in mind Nietzsche's understanding of the illusory nature of redemption and the possibility of joy as the deepest response to life, we may be able to understand the celebrational character of this poem and of much of Crane's poetry. It is generally said that Crane writes about the thwarted striving after some absolute ideal of beauty and love in the hopeless situation of modern man. I believe that this evaluation fails to do justice to the subtlety of Crane's work and carries with it a profound misapprehension of Romanticism in general. Statements of this sort, which speak of "Platonic ideals," clearly place Crane in an intellectual tradition with which he has little or no affinity, the pre-Romantic ethics of compensation and ultimate justice. No, Crane's poetry, and most

White Buildings: *The Character of Crane's Lyric*

illustratively "For the Marriage of Faustus and Helen," discredits remorse and pity, offering for irremediable loss neither consolation nor an imaginable hope for the future. In order to understand how such poetry can support its frequent tone of ecstatic enthusiasm, we must have some idea of how Romantic ideology developed, as I have been discussing in reference to Nietzsche, beyond the alternatives of optimism and pessimism.

The first matter to consider from this point of view, then, is the ambiguous character of Helen in the poem. We should recall that in Marlowe's play Helen is eminently desirable in a very physical, this-worldly fashion. She is "ideal" only in the sense that she is the woman Faustus would rather have above all others living or dead. But we should also recall that she is not a real woman in the play but a ghost, possibly even a devil in disguise; and, Faustus' choosing to conjure her up, just as his choosing every earthly value in the play, commits him to his original disavowal of God and his acceptance of death and damnation. To imagine a marriage, then, between Faustus and Helen represents a final, incontrovertible decision to pursue values, or valuable objects, without expecting consolation for their loss. Helen in this way becomes a symbol for the always equivocal experience of value, which is at the same time transcendental and illusory.

This double aspect of the sense of value is further brought out in the quotation from Jonson. Dol Common at this point in *The Alchemist* is duping Sir Epicure Mammon by feigning a mystic trance as these high-flown formulae are uttered. These lines express the same extravagant and ultimately futile hope that Helen represents for Faustus, but in an ironic light. So the title of the poem and its opening epigraph present human motivation as at once glorious and ridiculous. We saw that Crane was fascinated by this same tension in the Pierrot figure of Laforgue and that he incorporated it into his portrayal of Chaplin. This is a tension which he never allows to resolve completely either in the direction of euphoria or despair. Thus it is significant that this poem celebrates a marriage that has not occurred and that never can occur. One experiences value only as it is embodied in specific situations and goals; later one may look back on experience with detachment, even amusement, and wonder why it seemed so awesome at the time. Neither point of view vitiates the other. One may both take life seriously and find it absurd, but not at the same time.

So Helen, I believe, stands for more than beauty in the poem. She represents the experience of value, the feeling of meaningfulness which we call motivation, whether it be expressed in Wordsworth's "admiration, hope, and love" or in envy, lust, and hatred. As parts II and III of the poem reveal, the qualities of life being affirmed do not correspond to traditional moral interpretations of it. The sense of value means in part the ability to make moral decisions, but it also means the ability to contradict oneself in moral decisions and to justify virtually any action.

The poet defines his own position *vis-à-vis* the sense of value in part I, his hymn to Helen. The most important point to grasp in this section is that he not only responds powerfully to Helen but that he also continually examines what she means to him and how that meaning is taking place. In other words, value has become self-conscious for the poet; he grasps the contradictions concealed in his own experience and the price he pays for meaningfulness together with its hazards. His position is defined in contrast to the way value functions ordinarily in the lives of most men and in the lives of all men most of the time. This is the subject of the first two stanzas, the world of social roles, of policed behavior, and of concealed contradictions and inadequacies. It is a world filled with the everyday facts of life, the clichés of the working and playing day through which, as the last lines of the first stanza suggest, we occasionally feel that something is not quite right. One point needs to be made about the word "accepted" in line three. The meaning of that first sentence is not that the multitudes accept the oversimple norms of society. It is rather that the individual mind is too often disposed to accept generalized appearances as the norms by which it measures its

White Buildings: *The Character of Crane's Lyric*

own personal experience. For a person living by these standards it is the temporary and occasional relief of forgetfulness, in which problems are simply ignored and everything seems to fit together, that makes life endurable.

The transitional indented stanza in italics is the key to understanding how the poet's attitude toward value differs from the attitude he has just described.

> *There is the world dimensional for*
> *those untwisted by the love of things*
> *irreconcilable . . .*

This stanza has two important implications: first, that the categorical stability of the world, its dimensionality, is the product of a mind which is undisturbed by its own contradictory allegiances; and second, that a personal crisis in which one's values come into irreconcilable conflict jeopardizes that categorical stability, indeed sometimes precipitates the loss of that sense of the external world's reality. The rest of this section explores the poet's understanding of the sense of value and his relationship to the feeling of meaningfulness with a full awareness of its tenuous and equivocal nature. The next stanzas dramatize the psychological discipline presented earlier in "Legend"; the poet's self-conscious relationship to Helen is a stripping away of the masks which give value the illusion of permanence and externality.

Crane dramatizes his own state of mind as he begins this process of unmasking. The first sentence of stanza four describes a loss of orientation, in which directions and goals no longer exert any control over the poet.

> And yet, suppose some evening I forgot
> The fare and transfer, yet got by that way
> Without recall,—lost yet poised in traffic.
> Then I might find your eyes across an aisle,
> Still flickering with those prefigurations—
> Prodigal, yet uncontested now,
> Half-riant before the jerky window frame.

Vision of the Voyage

He is lost in the traffic without fare, but he does not care. Since he is no longer interested in where he is going or what he is about to do, he can look at what is around him in a wholly new way. It is at this point that he first can see those prodigal eyes across the aisle. And it is significant that those eyes are not immediately identified as Helen's. They are "really" the eyes of an anonymous young girl in the streetcar, but the frame of mind Crane now indulges makes it possible for the "meaning" of those eyes to change for him. They become an occasion for the experience of value without any commitment to specific action. In other words, they are a symbol for the sense of value itself, regardless of the problem situation in which it is expressed. The mythological dimension of this figure in the streetcar and the hymnlike, religious tone of this first section support the poet's endeavor to separate and celebrate value as an independent phenomenon. To do this the same insouciance toward the world is required that we saw before in "Legend." The image of the poet's love at the end of the fifth stanza, noncommittal as moonlight falling on snow, also recalls the "white falling flakes" of the earlier poem. What distinguishes the poet's emotional life from the frame of mind described in the first two stanzas is his willingness to let the dimensionality of his world, its recognizable and predictable quality, dissolve while he briefly stops struggling with the value conflicts he experiences every day. In this way he is able to celebrate value itself.

We should recall "Possessions" when reading the sixth stanza, which begins "Reflective conversion of all things." In that poem Crane isolated all the thrilling personal sensations of sexual encounters from the agonizing syndrome in which he had to experience them. He could praise one and hate the other. In this stanza Helen again represents that pure experience. Crane associates it with the annihilation of the world and with the void which is pictured surrounding the earth. What could be imagined as a catastrophe is here, though, an object of beauty. Value, since it is a way of responding, is really independent of the circumstances and consequences surrounding the valued object. The experience of value demands that we ignore many of these circumstances, sometimes even if they are vital.

The word "diaphanous" in stanza seven ("The world may glide diaphanous to death") is puzzling until we realize that it is in the mind that the earth is gliding to death or losing its reality. Matters that were before all-important become transparent, as it were, when a new focus on experience is achieved. Moreover, the sense of value is tyrannous. Stanza seven suggests that the ordinary shifting of goals and loyalties necessary in everyday life tends to vitiate the feeling of meaningfulness. Therefore, the poet imagines Helen captured by the Trojans, yet free and self-possessed in her own mind; it is in such a state, self-possession in a sustained and flexible irony, that the poet too can reach Helen. But Crane never says that he possesses Helen or reaches any consummation with her. Their relationship is like that of the two selves in "Recitative." It is a relationship which by its nature requires a sustained tension. Understanding how value operates, as Crane is doing in this poem, threatens the very experience of value. Value is an aesthetic phenomenon which masks and justifies action that in itself is meaningless. Penetrating the masks of value makes action impossible and is thus self-defeating. So Crane is reverent yet detached in his attitude toward Helen in the last stanza. And if we can grasp this paradoxical conception of value we can suggest a relationship between the three parts of the poem.

Part II contains in its first two stanzas one of the best examples in Crane's poetry of the stylization of experience. Crane shows no interest in the dancers on the roof garden except as patterns of light and rhythm; these stanzas are famous for their approximation in poetry of a jazz idiom. It is not important who is addressed in stanza three; in fact the anonymity reinforces the sense of detachment from all aspects of the scene except the aesthetic ones. The poet's advice to his companion, or perhaps even to himself, is that this frame of mind can be carried beyond the roof

Vision of the Voyage

garden. Thus the people sitting downstairs in the lobby form part of an orderly picture in which the poet plays no part. There is no consideration at all of choice or action here or on the roof, for the sense of value is being totally controlled by the poet. He is creating and sustaining a mask for reality. But the important point is that he knows it is a mask, and now in the fourth stanza he begins a kind of valuational experiment in which he tests this mask against the reality which cries out to be morally interpreted—war, or specifically the memory of having caused the destruction of human beings.

We may say that the first three stanzas demonstrate how all experiences of value occur or how one sees any object as valuable—by filtering experiences through a highly selective style of apprehension. It is really the style, the constantly reinforced pattern of cognitive gratification, that is "valuable." This becomes horribly apparent in the last two stanzas of this section where the poet construes the war experience as a stylistic pattern consonant with the dance scene above. The actual agony and destruction is clearly visible through the stylization, but the poet chooses to be "reassured" by the music at the end of the fourth stanza, to concentrate on the source of value, the style, rather than on some possibly unsettling aspects of the reality. Thus guilt is not honestly felt; it too becomes stylized, as a sweet, melancholy tune is played on the phonograph in the last stanza.

Part II hovers on the verge of a terrible awareness that is implicit in the equivocal treatment of value in part I. This awareness is made explicit in part III. Crane realizes that value is the result of the mind's continuing struggle to redeem a world which is characterized by destruction and irremediable loss. He personifies death on that dark road narrowing toward the dawn as the "arbiter of beauty." Without death, or the destructive aspect of becoming, there would be no need for beauty or value, which are responses of the mind always *in excess of* the data it operates upon. If the meaning of a configuration were commensurate with the configuration itself there could be no response and no beauty.

White Buildings: *The Character of Crane's Lyric*

But this is not the case; the mind is forever overreaching the world in order to defeat its sense of dissolution. Death is thus a "religious gunman" because it is at once the destroyer and the source of value for the living. Death should be understood also in its broadest sense as the loss of categorical predictability due to the ceaseless, chaotic flux of phenomena.

In part I Crane embarks on a quest for the sense of value because he is "twisted by the love of things irreconcilable." In parts II and III he dramatizes this divided state of mind by casting himself in the role of fighter pilot who has survived the war and who remembers the catastrophes he had a part in effecting. A rational optimism is no longer possible for him. He has penetrated this mask. So in part II he can consider what value really is—a stay against a guilt which is inescapable in a world filled with moral contradictions, a guilt which would incapacitate the individual if allowed to fester. Part II has the character of suspended decision. Here it is as if the speaker were intentionally postponing his encounter with more moral conundrums, especially with the one which plagues him most. But in part III he faces his memories of the war with a new awareness, and he no longer feels trapped between the alternatives of complicity and repentance. Crane rejects tragedy as a moral reconciliation of man with his fate.

Part III is a passionately felt reordering of experience. Nothing can erase, as stanzas three through six make clear, the actual facts of what occurred in World War I; the horror and beauty of the spectacle of death cannot be forgotten or explained. I understand stanza six ("We did not ask for that, but have survived") as a resolution not to forget what has been lived through in the war, not to find ways to justify and sentimentalize the atrocities. Helen—the sense of value—is of no help in such a resolution. She does not care if man destroys himself in pursuit of her. The kind of transcendental authority associated with the sense of value is quite beyond morality, and indeed beyond "the good of man." What man values can as easily destroy as preserve him: Helen's gifts are "blessing and dismay."

Stanza seven links the sense of value with the symbol-making process. The point about the collection "goose, tobacco and cologne" is that virtually anything can become an object of great value for man. The mythological imagination redeems existence, staves off despair, by sanctifying whatever is at hand. A poignancy can be added to these lines if one knows that Crane saw these three objects listed in a newspaper article recounting a crime. They were all the thief managed to get away with.[18]

Anchises and Erasmus are heroes in the poem because they both looked back on fallen worlds—Troy and scholasticism—but at the same time were laying the foundations for new civilizations. The next lines in stanza seven are, I believe, an apostrophe to death, and they are spoken with the same reverence as the lines addressed to Helen in part I.

> Delve upward for the new and scattered wine,
> O brother-thief of time, that we recall.

They emphasize the importance of forgetfulness in the creation of a new order. Then Crane appeals to death to scorn those who are not able to accept loss and failure for what they are, but who must justify them with an always inadequate penance. The last lines of this stanza are a painfully acute moral condemnation of Philistinism and should dispel once and for all any "idealistic" reading of the figure of Helen in the poem. They say that people should be ashamed not to acknowledge the suffering and waste which are the price of their own values. It is not even for a real bodily Helen of Troy that men will destroy each other and themselves, but for a mere token of the original, for the weakest pretense to meaningfulness: "For golden, or the shadow of gold hair." The

---

[18]R. W. B. Lewis, *The Poetry of Hart Crane, A Critical Study* (Princeton: Princeton University Press, 1967), p. 115, n. 20.

White Buildings: *The Character of Crane's Lyric*

full irony of Dol Common's speech from *The Alchemist* can now be appreciated.

But we must be careful in trying to describe the tone, or tones, of "Faustus and Helen," for we never hear cynicism or even disillusionment. It is a celebrational lyric which does justice to a highly equivocal conception of the sense of value. While demonstrating that "moral integrity"—the reconciliation of the sense of value with rational optimism—is an illusion, Crane nevertheless celebrates life unredeemed. The implication of the last stanza is that man finds his joy not in attempting to justify the past or in attempting to mold the future into a predictable happiness, but in responding to phenomena's challenge to create meaning anew.

> Distinctly praise the years, whose volatile
> Blamed bleeding hands extend and thresh the height
> The imagination spans beyond despair,
> Outpacing bargain, vocable and prayer.

Crane refers to a number of poets and writers in his poetry. And they usually serve, like Anchises and Erasmus in "Faustus and Helen," a kind of mythological function. We have seen that later generations of Romantic poets create from the lives and works of their predecessors a hagiology which supports and guides them in their own alienation. In this respect Whitman was, it is often said, Crane's patron saint, but too great an emphasis on Whitman as a model for reading Crane's poetry badly distorts it. For balance we should bear in mind Herman Melville, with whom Crane also had a strong intellectual affinity. Remembering Crane's elegy to Ernest Nelson, though, we should recall that it is not the person himself or his specific works and opinions that are beatified. No, one may speak of a "Romantic tradition" only as a methodology or a psychology that serves as the basis for interpreting experience and writing poetry. Melville certainly did his part in exploring that psychology. Perhaps his greatest contribution was the symbology he created from the sea. Together with his interest in the mask-like character of reality, this sym-

Vision of the Voyage

bolization of the sea as the phenomenal world, which man confronts at his own risk, is his chief bequest to Crane.

The point emphasized about the sea in "At Melville's Tomb" is that it swallows up men and ships, leaving only the vaguest hints to survivors about the lives of the dead. Melville represents for Crane the man who sees this process without sentimentality or justifying illusions. More specifically, he is the man who can face the dissolution of categorical knowledge and at the same time suspend his interpretation of what that knowledge was about and of what its loss means. It is the confrontation with irremediable loss that is the beginning and the real test of Romanticism.

The focus of the poem is trained on the purely exemplary aspects of the catastrophe, not on any moral interpretation of it. The poem's effectiveness rests on sustained synecdoche. The sailors become only bones, dice in a ghostly crap game which the sea always wins. They become anonymous numbers as individuals are scattered like sand or waves. The sound of bells would give to their passing some social or religious significance, but the only meaning allowed them is the indecipherable pattern of whatever floats to the surface after the ship has sunk. The meaning is no more articulate than the roar in a sea shell. The third stanza implies that what cries out for interpretation is not the facts of death at sea but man's predisposition for answers.

> Then in the circuit calm of one vast coil,
> Its lashings charmed and malice reconciled,
> Frosted eyes there were that lifted altars;
> And silent answers crept across the stars.

In order to comprehend the world man sets it apart from himself, so to speak, as an other. Paradoxically it is the tension between man and the world, the irreconcilability of categorical knowledge and experience, that makes comprehension possible. Therefore when the sea bridges the gap between man and the world, no categorical knowledge is possible or needed. "Lashings" and "malice" are functions of the mind's alienation from the world.

White Buildings: *The Character of Crane's Lyric*

The reconciliation of man and the world is the annihilation of thought. So the answers creeping across the stars are not mysterious; the answers are silence. Eyes that cannot see look toward apocalypse; instruments can no longer *make* the world they measure; and there is no one to hear the complaint of death. The last line refers not only to Melville, but to every person lost at sea and to every categorical object, which must eventually lose its reality.

Crane's greatest exploration of the nature of meaning, besides *The Bridge,* is the set of six poems dealing with love and the sea called "Voyages." Their subject is the glory of the experience of value in the world and the impossibility of sustaining it. It is generally said that these poems record the history of a love affair which in "Voyages V" disintegrates because of the unfaithfulness either of the beloved or of the poet. But the "piracy" referred to in that poem is something more inevitable than infidelity. The dilemma these poems explore is the central problem in the psychology I have been discussing, the unavoidable breakdown of categorical knowledge with the onslaught of phenomena.

The first poem in this series introduces the conception of the sea which Crane found in Melville. It represents the phenomenal world which, seen from a protected point of view, seems manageable and attractive, but which, entered upon, is uncontrollably destructive. To the children playing on the beach the sea is no more than a backdrop for their little game. But part of its real nature is introduced in stanza two, in which the weak voices of the children are swallowed up in the roar made by the sea on the beach. The poet cannot actually give the children the advice he would like. The children represent a frame of mind unaware of the dangers of its own experience. Experience cannot counsel innocence; they are mutually exclusive. For when one is convinced of the predictability and manageability of the world, no threat seems real. And when chaos begins to intrude, the old innocence seems to have been an illusion. Crane is concerned

Vision of the Voyage

with two aspects of the sea. The first is an extension of the human imagination: the promise of love, the sea's charismatic fascination. The other is the sea's incompatibility with man's desires and expectations, its vastness, and thus, from man's point of view, its cruelty.

"Voyages II" begins to chart the imaginative involvement of the mind with the world in love. This experience of Romantic ecstasy embodies the tyrannous and enthralling sense of value within some objectification of reality and protects the resulting symbol by the distortion of the rest of experience. The sea is the perfect setting for the dramatization of such an imaginative grasp of reality. For, isolated in such vastness, the mind seems to be limitlessly powerful. The sea in this poem thus supports the totalistic structure the world is receiving as it is redeemed by the imagination. Nothing about the vast power of the sea is seen to contradict or limit the experience of love. In fact it is as if this love were the one point at which all the forces of the world conjoined in harmony. The sea is like a body to the moon's love in stanza one, and the destructive aspects of her power judiciously grant amnesty to love alone. The entire perceptual world cooperates in the famous stanza three to create a pattern of harmonious movement in which the secret passion of the lovers is the axis.

> And onward, as bells off San Salvador
> Salute the crocus lustres of the stars,
> In these poinsettia meadows of her tides,—
> Adagios of islands, O my Prodigal,
> Complete the dark confessions her veins spell.

Crane used "adagios of islands" to illustrate his "logic of metaphor."[19] This image exploits the ambiguity of sense experience, illustrating how the redemption of the world actually occurs. One would ordinarily place the sense of movement in the

---

[19] "General Aims and Theories," *The Complete Poems*, p. 221.

White Buildings: *The Character of Crane's Lyric*

ship as it drifts slowly among islands, but Crane displaces the movement so that an illusion of personal control over perception is experienced. The islands glide slowly by, and their movement reinforces the symbolism of the clandestine riches of his desire.

In the fourth stanza we get a hint of the precarious quality of this ecstasy.

> Mark how her turning shoulders wind the hours,
> And hasten while her penniless rich palms
> Pass superscription of bent foam and wave,—
> Hasten, while they are true,—sleep, death, desire,
> Close round one instant in one floating flower.

The meaning of that superscription the sea writes in foam and wave must be grasped quickly while it lasts. And it is really only one instant of apprehension that is symbolized in the floating flower. That symbol of the love experience, or of the imaginative experience in general, contains two-thirds annihilation and one-third will. It is above all the negation of incompatible responses that gives this love its power and joy. Thus the last stanza appeals for a continuation of the voyage at sea, where the perceptual world is most ambiguous, most susceptible to the imagination. The poet would have that voyage end in the complete surrender of poet and beloved to their own symbolic world in a whirlpool death. Only there can the apocalyptic union of man, nature, and imagination occur. This poem is a *Liebestod* worthy of comparison with Wagner.

"Voyages III" is a further exploration into the psychology of love. It is a wonderful evocation of the way a valued object or person can supply a set of interpretive models for the rest of experience. The categorical flexibility required in problem solving can be replaced by an obsessive concern for associations with the valued object. As we saw in the preceding poem, the systematic negation of all responses incompatible with the state of ecstasy carries with it a very active sense of control and power. Here, though, in the next stage of this process, a sense of passivity

Vision of the Voyage

overtakes the poet. When a valued object commanding complete devotion supplies the stylistic principles for structuring and validating experience, one's feelings of self-determination are weakened. And if the process continues, the sense of personal identity, which arises from the tensions of problem solving rather than from their relaxation, will also be threatened.

The sea, then, in "Voyages III" becomes a mode of apprehending or contemplating the beloved. The sea and sky reenact the relationship of poet and beloved. The meaning of the last four lines of the first stanza is not so much that the poet is never far away from his beloved, as that he cannot be separated from him since the waves have become virtually the symbolic equivalent of his embraces.

> While ribboned water lanes I wind
> Are laved and scattered with no stroke
> Wide from your side, whereto this hour
> The sea lifts, also, reliquary hands.

The danger of such a state is implied in the last line. The sea, which was seen in "Voyages I" as potentially destructive, is here capable of appearing only in devotional harmony with the valued object. By this point in the "Voyages" we begin to realize how great the discrepancy is between the phenomenal world and our stylistic modes of apprehending it, which are governed by the sense of value. The dangers of this discrepancy are implicit in the poem, and we have been instructed, so to speak, in how to see them by "Voyages I." The state of abandonment in love carries with it very much the same hazardous innocence that we saw in the children on the beach.

Notice that the long second stanza lacks both the first person pronoun and a main verb, and that it abounds in participles, giving the sense of being carried along by the currents and by passion. And something of the rapture of the experience and of the ignored danger is suggested by presenting the underwater world in architectural and fluid terms. Nothing is solid or safe

White Buildings: *The Character of Crane's Lyric*

about this building, but the poet sees only the play of light in the water and its erotic associations together with those of the rocking waves. The last four lines of this stanza mean that the only death in this world is the transformation of one reality into another, making possible the aesthetic redemption of the world in love.

> and where death, if shed,
> Presumes no carnage, but this single change,—
> Upon the steep floor flung from dawn to dawn
> The silken skilled transmemberment of song;

"Transmemberment" is a coined word which refers to the apprehension of one object under the aspect of another, for instance seeing the rocking waves as embraces or vice versa. It is the faculty of grasping that "infinite consanguinity" between the beloved and the sea. The poem ends in the total surrender of the poet to the beloved, or of the poet to his own now tyrannical stylistic mode of apprehension. The last line is not even an assertion but a plea: "Permit me voyage, love, into your hands . . . " It is as if those children of "Voyages I" began to swim out into the ocean.

"Voyages IV" is the turning point in the series. For there the dangers which were implicit in the two previous poems are realized, and the enthralling love relationship begins to be self-conscious. One is no longer carried along by the even cadences and rhetoric. It is as if the poet were struggling to think for himself again. He can now adopt a tentative attitude toward his experience and even question it. In other words what in "Voyages II" and "III" was a powerful immediate response has now become mediated; the poet's response has become a stimulus in its own right. This is not to say that the feelings of love have vanished, or that experience is any less transformed by those feelings. The difference is that the poet has become aware of them. He has grasped the discrepancy between the phenomenal world and his mode of apprehending it, and he begins to consider some of the implications of his new knowledge.

Vision of the Voyage

Time, not infidelity, makes this knowledge possible. The "repetition" of responses finally results in an intellectual distance from them in a kind of irony. Thus "Voyages IV" is a consideration of the relationship of time to the timeless sense of value. The disjointedness and convolutions of syntax suggest the straining of the mind toward self-consideration in the midst of the powerful love experience. The first phrase modifies "love" in the last line of the preceding poem. Let me offer this rough paraphrase for the first stanza. —Let us assume that our limited time together is symbolized to me by a rainbow on the sea and that I promise that the vastness of the sea and the flight of the bird represent no greater love, no more fusion of the timeless in the temporal, than our love for each other and my poetry about our love.— Of particular interest in this stanza is the symbolization of the feeling of meaningfulness by the arch of a bird's flight and the use of the verb "bridge" to mean the relationship of an individual to a valued object. We will return to these images in discussing the introductory poem of *The Bridge*. Here, though, let me suggest that responding to the flight of a bird as a thing of beauty is a demonstration of the mind's ability to imbue unsubstantial phenomena with reality and value. The curve of the bird's flight does not, strictly speaking, "exist" as a thing, just as no object of the mind really exists in the world. And Crane's symbol for the mind's continuing effort to imbue experience with value is the bridge.

The word play in the second stanza suggests that Crane is regaining a sense of control over his feelings. He is able to call the logic of mutual possession "mad." And he seems to be distancing himself from his emotional absorption through synecdoche. Thought is exerting itself over feeling. The power the senses exert over each other, as a smell brings to mind the eyes and lips of the beloved, is now seen as contingent upon the wills of poet and beloved. They can repeat erotic experiences which sanctify small amounts of time or not, as they choose. And in the next stanza the poet asks if the symbols for the timeless moments,

White Buildings: *The Character of Crane's Lyric*

recalling the "one floating flower" of "Voyages II," will not take on a merely temporal quality after the period of ecstasy. Notice too in the last line of stanza three that Crane is fully aware of the price he has paid for the highly valued experience which produced those symbols.

Recall that in "Voyages II" the desire to sustain feelings of intense meaningfulness was represented by the hope never to see land again. But now in the fourth stanza the harbor appears. And the poet can unmask, as it were, his own love experience. As in "Possessions" he realizes that the meaning of that experience lies really in the gratifying repetition of fantasy. The eyes of the beloved and their effect upon the poet's experience have been a synopsis of that fantasy life. Again emphatic light imagery accompanies the breakdown of the illusion and of the meaningfulness. The last two lines are addressed to the beloved, urging him to accept love as it is newly understood, as requiring a mask and being a temporary redemption of the personality in fantasy.

> In this expectant, still exclaim receive
> The secret oar and petals of all love.

The last line, then, does not refer narrowly to the clandestine nature of Crane's affair, but to the protective mask required by all love.

By "Voyages V," the mask of love has been stripped away. The poet's most cherished object, his beloved, is now seen to have been a symbol through which a thorough mediation of his experience had taken place. The sheer diversity of his own responses and the discrepancy he has discovered between the ambiguous external world and his highly valued style of apprehending it has led him to see the value of his beloved as tenuous and contingent upon his own will. So he has rediscovered his own freedom in spite of what he loves most. And this recovery of himself, as we see in the first three stanzas of "Voyages V," puts the external world in a whole new perspective. Lucidity is gained by the penetration of masks. The poet is able now to look at the

Vision of the Voyage

bay carefully and to see the sharp definition of water and sky. Its objectivity seems stable and uncompromising, implying an irresolvable separation between the poet and what he sees. In this state of estrangement from the beloved and from the world previously inhabited, the moonlight is unsympathetic, indeed incapable of sympathy, and the poet would blot it out altogether rather than see it as a mockery of his imagination. Actually the moonlight and his imagination were no less tyrannous in the love relationship than they are now, but since the poet's surrender to them is over, his alienation from this symbol in stanza three is particularly oppressive. For he knows how inevitable the loss of meaningfulness is and why it must occur: he has watched it happen in his own heart.

It is clear in stanzas four and five that the beloved has not gone through the same education in the psychology of love that the poet has. The beloved utters a sentimental commonplace about the scene before them, "There's/Nothing like this in the world," to which the poet cannot respond sympathetically. In "Voyages II" and "III" the poet could have touched his beloved's hand and looked into a world transformed by sympathetic beauty and love; now he sees only an empty, unanimated universe.

> Knowing I cannot touch your hand and look
> Too, into that godless cleft of sky
> Where nothing turns but dead sands flashing.

The beloved's "And never to quite understand!" is highly ironic at this point. He means that we can never understand how this beauty before us is possible. But from the poet's point of view, the beloved can never understand what has transpired between them. This failure of the beloved to understand makes communication between them impossible. And worse, the poet understands now that the previous "communication" had really only been the temporary narrowing of his entire world to a symbology based on the beloved. The piracy, then, is the unavoidable betrayal of our values by the world or by our own continuing

White Buildings: *The Character of Crane's Lyric*

responses. But as we saw in "Faustus and Helen," Crane does not deny value in light of the phenomenal world. He celebrates the value-making process without surrendering his equivocal conception of specific values and his ironic attitude toward them. So we see him continuing to be gentle with his beloved in the last stanza, although the poet's world and his beloved's are no longer compatible. The poet can see the beloved's eyes in the drifting foam, but now as if they were floating away about to vanish. They are strangers to each other now, so there is nothing more to do but return to land.

The subtlety of the "Voyages" sequence results from Crane's use of the sea to record the experience of love and its loss. It is never merely the beloved which is celebrated in these poems; the abundance of love is found in the infinite ambiguity of the world, for which the sea is a symbol. In fact, we may say that the poet's willingness to engage in a dialectic with the sea, to admit and examine the confusion of his own feelings rather than to deceive himself in order to save the relationship, is what makes these poems so interesting. They fall within that genre which is a strange combination of the love poem and the elegy, of which Wordsworth's Lucy poems and Arnold's Switzerland series are examples. The poet considers his beloved, the heightened quality love has given his life and the intuition of mortality that it has also given him. Wordsworth identifies Lucy and love with the mind in its most revelatory state, when nonsocietal nature is the unequivocal mode of sensing pure meaningfulness. This state cannot be sustained indefinitely, so Lucy and love are also associated with death. And for Arnold the belief that "two human hearts might blend/In one" is only a dream.

Love begins by making life bearable, for it discovers the richness of the world touched by the imagination, and it discovers freedom in the prerogative of self-abandonment. But love ends by making life unbearable, for it also discovers the recalcitrance of the world and the freedom of the beloved to be himself. Love discovers that the heart is unsatisfied because it is insatiable. The

Vision of the Voyage

lover, in seeking to satisfy the heart, fails; but in the process he discovers himself, the world, and the beloved for the first time as they really are. And since life can be seen for what it is, it must be. The difficult and painful extrication of man from his own values is possible if he is willing to acknowledge the ambiguous and contradictory aspects of his own experience. He must commit himself to alienation and the penetration of masks. The loss of a highly validated personal identity and of a belief in the coherence of man with himself, man with man, and man with nature or God is the price he must pay for the corrigibility of the mind, for the constant rediscovery of freedom.

"Voyages VI" is a summing up and a celebration of all that has been learned from this love experience. It is an acceptance of the losses incurred through alienation, and an acceptance of phenomenal reality as the difficult cure for self-deception. The poem, like the conclusion of "Faustus and Helen," is also a hymn of praise to value, to the always new possibility of meaningfulness in experience.

The "place" described in the first two stanzas represents the poet's state of mind at the end of the love affair, as he regains his objectivity and considers his losses. He is at first overcome by the vastness of the world, which he has previously structured so completely and narrowly around his beloved. He is aware of the great world below the surface of the ocean, a dungeon for lost swimmers. And this world is strange to him with its underwater currents like rivers, whose movement is as continuous as the roar in a sea shell. The point at which sea and sky meet is identified with the phoenix, for the poet is able to imagine again the sense of value apart from specific values, especially from his beloved. But the poet dwells in the next lines and in stanza four on his own state, having lost what means most to him, his mode of apprehending the world as valuable. He is thus blind and without destination, waiting passionately for a new symbol of value but unable to define it.

Instead of looking for that symbol, accepting a revaluation of

White Buildings: *The Character of Crane's Lyric*

his experience right away, he postpones reentering his life, so to speak, in order fully to appreciate what he has learned. Let the world crash around me, he says in stanza four. For he is enjoying the rare feeling of insouciance which comes from realizing how tentative all values really are. In the midst of threatening or portentious experience it is finally the simple evasive movement (earlier a bird's flight) which captures most closely the character of the feeling of value. Like a cliff seen from a ship as it seems to swing by, or a sail seen from land on a clear April day, the sense of value now appears to the poet as a glance from the eyes of a sublimely indifferent goddess. And the last two stanzas praise the symbol-making power itself. "Belle Isle" is not so much the island off Newfoundland, but literally a beautiful island. Islands generally stand in these poems for some particular manifestation of value. Here the meaning is generalized into what Nietzsche called "eternal recurrence," the continual construing of the world, as long as life lasts, as meaningful.

The special character of Crane's lyrics was produced from a sensibility passionate and simple, by a mind as brilliant as Eliot's. Crane could glean from a magazine article or an offhand conversation the essence of a current of thought too advanced for most to grasp with the best education. His poetry begins with the complete and honest indulgence of personal feelings; then a most penetrating introspection pushes these toward what I have called absolute knowledge. The result is an intensely personal lyricism cast in the light of an awareness of the deceiving nature of thought and feeling themselves. But neither the feeling nor the awareness is surrendered. Crane's difficult style is his solution to the problem of sustaining tension between the two. It involves exploiting the ambiguity of sense experience under the direction of the sense of value. His willingness to destroy the comfortable individuation and public aspect of experience results in a Dionysian art which rejects optimism but transcends pessimism. And it results in a uniquely Romantic lyric which celebrates life without pretending to correct existence. His poetry is thus unabashedly personal, confessional, proud, and relentlessly self-conscious.

There can be no arbitration, I suppose, between this understanding of Crane's art and the moral condemnations of the anti-Romantic critics. Allen Tate is perhaps the most eloquent of these,[20] and his accusations of puerility and confusion carry with them a rejection of the whole intellectual tradition I have been discussing. It is ironic to me that such criticism condemns Crane as irresponsible in failing to achieve moral "definition" and to produce a tragic art. For from the Romantic point of view, it is the failure to acknowledge the *limitations* of moral definitions and the discrepancy between them and experience that courts disaster. What is the price of rational optimism?

---

[20]See his two essays, "Hart Crane" and "Crane: The Poet as Hero" in *Collected Essays* (Denver: Allan Swallow, 1959), pp. 225-237, 528-532. Tate sums up Romanticism in this way: " . . . instead of the effort to define himself in the midst of almost overwhelming complications—a situation that might have produced a tragic poet—he (Crane) falls back upon the intensity of consciousness, rather than the clarity, for his center of vision. And that is romanticism."

3

The Bridge:
The Meaning of Suffering

We see from the epigraph on the title page that *The Bridge* is a poem about suffering. These lines from *The Book of Job—From going to and fro in the earth, / and from walking up and down in it.* —are spoken by Satan, who represents the Byronic perspective of exiled consciousness. Repentance and obedience have been precluded by his fall, so he must see the world without hope or consolation. The perspective of the fallen angel, a hero to earlier Romantics, prepares us for Crane's voyage through human experience, not the perspective of Job. We need to understand how the trials of Job differ from the experiences Crane will present in the following poems. The strength and salvation of Job rest in his continuing effort to trust in ultimate justice in the face of overwhelming disappointment. The series of losses Job experiences in no way invalidates for him the one Value which he serves in spite of the Devil and the world. Indeed this is just the point. Job is saved *in spite of* suffering, not *through* suffering. The tension between the Good and the circumstances of his existence becomes *almost* unbearable, but never completely so, for faith sustains him. Job is not any wiser at the end of the book than he is at the beginning; he has known everything needful for his deliverance all along. It is obedience which is extolled.

Vision of the Voyage

Critics might as well be said to have modeled their understanding of Crane's suffering on Job's. They have replaced Job's faith in God with some ideal, again a Platonic one, to which Crane has access. And they have replaced the vicissitudes of the world with a disappointing contemporary America—industrialism, mythic poverty, Philistinism—incompatible with the poet's vision and faith. They seem to feel that *The Bridge* should be judged as a narrative poem, an epic, which attempts to justify such an idealism and make it viable once more for America by symbolizing it in modern terms, specifically in terms of the Brooklyn Bridge. They conclude, though, that since this justification never seems to take place—no satisfying modern religion emerges—and that since the relationship of the poems to each other in light of such a plan is hazy at best, *The Bridge* is a failure ideologically and poetically.[1]

Critics of *The Bridge* speak as if Crane, like Job, were only waiting to be proved right in his struggle with the world. Such a judgment implies an awful spiritual complacency and self-

---

[1] One of the earliest and most influential statements of these opinions is Yvor Winters' "The Significance of *The Bridge* by Hart Crane, or What Are We to Think of Professor X?" in his *In Defense of Reason* (Denver: University Press, 1943), pp. 575-603. Among later critics there is an amazing consistency in the assumptions and biases which they share with Winters, although he would have labelled each of them "Professor X," a naive admirer of Emerson and Whitman. See Brom Weber's *Hart Crane* (New York: Bodley Press, 1948), L. S. Dembo's *Hart Crane's Sanskrit Charge: A Study of "The Bridge"* (Ithaca: Cornell University Press, 1960), Samuel Hazo's *Hart Crane* (New York: Barnes and Noble, 1963), Vincent Quinn's *Hart Crane* (New York: Twayne Publishers, 1963), and R. W. B. Lewis' *The Poetry of Hart Crane* (Princeton: Princeton University Press, 1967). Common to these critics is a notion of the "visionary" which obscures the psychology of Crane's poetry and which carries with it the seeds of Winters' condemnation. Recently, however, two studies have appeared which avoid this assumption: Sherman Paul's helpful and thorough *Hart's Bridge* (Urbana: University of Illinois Press, 1972) and M. D. Uroff's *Hart Crane: The Patterns of His Poetry* (Urbana: University of Illinois Press, 1974).

The Bridge: *The Meaning of Suffering*

righteousness which are utterly out of character with the poem. Their mistake comes really from their own assumption that values, ideals, and the Good for man in whatever symbolic form it takes, are always at odds with falseness, evil, and the world, and that the good man can save himself and effect beneficial changes in society by identifying himself with the former and resisting the latter. These assumptions compose the psychology Hegel called the "unhappy consciousness," which cultivates the distant possibility of solutions to present unsolvable problems. The faith of asceticism in the next world is Hegel's example of this psychology. Crane's Romantic idealism does not rely on assumptions like these.

Romanticism, in fact, destroyed the foundations of such a metaphysic. By approaching the sense of value phenomenologically the Romantics tore the feeling of meaningfulness away from the sphere of personal and social management, where the opposition of good and evil actually resides. Therefore the struggles of a Romantic—and his suffering—are not in attempting to define and maintain goodness against evil in his age, but in tearing himself apart as a cultural product. He understands that his own joy, what in spite of everything makes life worth living, is always prior to and independent of definition. Every specific cultural value represents an attempt to make that yes-saying to experience manageable and permanent. And it is this pretense to permanence, this constant masking of experience in the service of rational optimism, which he feels compelled to penetrate. He does this not out of any high calling or because of any special faculty but because he loves cultural masks too well himself. Instead of using them as others do, with a nonchalant hypocrisy and never a backward glance, he gives them his fidelity and belief, only to be disappointed by them and bewildered by the irrationality and pessimistic cast of his own experience. I see no attempt in *The Bridge* to supply anything needful to the spiritual life of Americans; the poem speaks only to a few and it does everything but save them. The poem records the struggles and

Vision of the Voyage

sufferings of a man who saw everywhere around him and within himself the failure of life-forces to take on any permanently meaningful form. Crane penetrates, one after another, the hopes he would like to feel in institutions and conceptualizations. He finds every value to contain a dimension of pathos as it is seen to be an ultimately futile attempt to master the phenomenal world.

But Crane's vision, as we have seen, is not morbid. For every valuational interpretation of experience, however futile and foolish it ultimately is, has a sovereignty and glory within the limitations it sets for itself. The beautiful world of appearances, even the beauty of delusion and intoxication, forms the largest part of the fabric of the poem. Yet Crane's focus of attention and interpretation widens and narrows, so that we are never allowed to succumb to any of the "answers" implicit in the material of each section. Also, different stylistic principles operate in each poem, so the illusion of narrator-identity is successfully avoided. Indeed if we must find a source of narrative continuity, it is in just this flexibility of perspective. For the mind is represented in this poem not by identifying it with certain values as it struggles to oppose their negation, but by representing the external world in all its richness and ambiguity, in all its contradictory aspects as cultural values structure it, dissolve, and reappear in new forms. We might say that the mind of the narrator presented in these lyrics is like a great movie screen on which all tableaux possible in his culture can be seen and eventually seen through. The meaning of the screen and the play of lights is problematical, but the beauty and fascination of the characters and plots are never denied. As in "Faustus and Helen" it is the eternal possibility of meaningfulness, in whatever circumstances, that is celebrated in *The Bridge*.

All the implications of the Brooklyn Bridge as a central symbol in the poem can be appreciated only after a thorough reading of the lyrics. But the introductory poem "To Brooklyn Bridge" contains in miniature much of the whole poem's sweep and multifariousness. Notice first that the poem does not begin

The Bridge: *The Meaning of Suffering*

with the Bridge itself, but with the flight of a seagull. The first three stanzas expand this image, until the sudden, evasive movement comes to stand for thought itself, especially for the freedom of the mind and its forgetfulness. A daydream or a glimpse of a sail only briefly interrupts the work of a clerk, and the last sudden movement of his day removes the whole office world from him. Perhaps he goes to a movie where he, like everyone else there, can forget all but the magic on the screen which seems to promise some important message or a prophecy. What unites everyone in the theater is their hope of finding something of value there. This scene recalls "Faustus and Helen I"; the movie house could easily be that "somewhere/Virginal perhaps, less fragmentary, cool." So the poem begins by suggesting that people lead their lives among evasive, equivocal meanings. And the poet sees the flight of the seagull over New York Harbor as symbolic of the action of their minds.

Then he turns to Brooklyn Bridge, which he sees as the expression of a paradox. The Bridge is both powerful movement and repose. In contemplating it the mind leaps back and forth between the two notions, unsure which to admire more. We may say that the Bridge represents the eternal (therefore constant) possibility of movement. Or to put it in psychological terms, the Bridge suggests the Hegelian notion of *aufheben,* which means both to preserve or lift up and to negate. Movement, purely considered, is only negation: moving from a to b negates a, for one moves to not-a. But the Bridge stands for more than negation or movement. It means as well the consideration of movement as a process, or, to use another Hegelian phrase, the negation of the negation. It stands for the prerogative to respond to one's own responses, to estrange oneself from one's own thoughts and actions, so that they become not determining patterns but objects in themselves whose meaning is temporarily problematical. Through this process thought becomes self-conscious, as a mask is penetrated and action is for a while impossible. Under this aspect of knowledge one's motivations lose their power and one's

Vision of the Voyage

valuational interpretations seem shallow and artificial. The world in its most destructive moments may thus be seen as blamelessly indifferent.

In stanza five Crane describes a suicide on the Bridge callously received by a busy public. The man who is jumping from the Bridge and the people who joke about him are both being hurled along by the unself-conscious patterns of thought symbolized earlier by the bird's flight. Notice that the motion in both images imitates the dip of the gull's wing. Values in Crane's poetry are tyrannical and make no concession to consistency or even final outcome. But the Bridge looms over the scene uncommitted to both actions. Stanza seven emphasizes that the Bridge's mysterious blessing to man is forgetfulness. Time is generally feared because it bestows anonymity, but here time is presented as attempting to *defeat* anonymity. In other words, through time and memory actions in the past are justified and take on a reality they do not deserve. But the Bridge defeats these superstitious efforts of the mind. It grants anonymity and thus reprieve. The only *real,* as opposed to *aesthetic,* redemption of the world is in the mind's ability to forget everything.

Stanza eight ("O harp and altar, of the fury fused") suggests that values, utterances of love and hope, are born from the Bridge, from the paradoxes of desire and futility, pride and anonymity. The transformation of a chaotic, destructive world into a meaningful, gratifying one can occur because of the mind's two powers: to forget or negate almost all of experience and to lift out of its past a few moments, preserving and sanctifying them. The Brooklyn Bridge symbolized to Crane these two processes working together.

In the last two stanzas Crane is turning away from the Bridge and is about to consider a great deal of experience, both historically significant and mundane. He is standing apart from the "caravan" on the Bridge and from the office workers. Standing in the Bridge's shadow, he watches night come on as little squares of light appear against the darkness of the buildings. The

The Bridge: *The Meaning of Suffering*

line "Only in darkness is thy shadow clear" means that only as the hectic abundance of sights and sounds is temporarily blotted out can the mind consider its own processes and know how it relates to the hectically abundant world. Looking for God in such a world, it must look through a myth that expresses what is feared most and understood least. In the Bridge's leaping, still curves it expresses prayers, cries, and silence. Crane says that it could lend a myth to God.

The idea of God in post-Romantic thinking means the hypostatized point at infinity toward which the mind moves as it approaches Absolute Knowledge. Absolute Knowledge refers to the mind's continual rediscovery of its own freedom through the mediation of its experience beyond the bondage of whatever cultural values limit and stabilize its categories. This process leads to continual reencounters with the phenomenal world and to a suspension of ultimate judgment about it. So the Bridge and its myth free the mind to see new possibilities for value and beauty.

Seeking new possibilities is a continuing theme of *The Bridge,* and we should begin with it in our discussion of "Ave Maria." The epigraph from *Medea* is spoken by the chorus which has been remembering the Argonauts' victory over the sea in uniting disparate lands. Now they look toward the future "to an age in the far-off years when Ocean shall unloose the bonds of things, when the whole broad earth shall be revealed, when Tethys (Jason's helmsman) shall disclose new worlds, and Thule shall no longer be the limit of the lands."[2] This speech is a prophecy of apocalypse which imagines a time in which man will have complete dominion over the earth. But if we read the following poem carefully we must realize that such a hope is only one part of the ambiguous relationship of Columbus to Cathay, Spain, and the sea.

In the first place, Columbus had not, as he thought, found Cathay. He says that being proved right nearly drove him mad

---

[2] Lewis, pp. 257-258.

Vision of the Voyage

with joy, but we know that he was *not* right. So we see the sense of value again as glorious and ridiculous. Columbus wants more than anything else for his success to be substantiated at the court of Ferdinand and Isabella. Columbus is like Job seen in an ironic light. For what matters to him is being justified by authority. He fully realizes his precarious situation on the sea; it would be easy for him to be swallowed up and forgotten. Crane uses the sea here to symbolize the phenomenal world. For Columbus associates time and space with his possible annihilation. He knows that he was actually there, in "Cathay," only a short time ago, but now the sun continues to set on that land without the least regard for his accomplishment. He imagines his position, threatened by the sea and possibly by mutiny, to be like that of Christianity, tenuously and miraculously protected from the infidels. That is, it is conceivable that the Moors could not only kill the physical bodies of Christians, but wipe out the very saving Word itself. Throughout this poem associations with the Incarnation, the Word made Flesh, define the importance Columbus gives to his mission. Stanza six ("Series on series, infinite,—till eyes") presents the apocalyptic vision which has been induced by being at sea so long without markers to provide a sense of relationships and limitations. And Columbus sounds really mad as he apostrophizes Fernando, warning him already against greed when the riches of Cathay become accessible. He goes on to hope, still with the apocalyptic imagination, that he will return to a war-free Spain.

Then, in the second half of the poem, Columbus turns to God in meditation and a prayer of praise. The emphasis in this section is upon the necessity of faith in carrying out God's incomprehensible plan. The phenomenal world is a revelation of this plan to the believer, so the paradoxes of existence can be suspended in faith. In stanza nine God is presented like the ocean, holding both birth and death, yet somehow apart from them, keeping the purpose behind them secret.

The Bridge: *The Meaning of Suffering*

O Thou who sleepest on Thyself, apart
Like ocean athwart lanes of death and birth,
And all the eddying breath between dost search
Cruelly with love thy parable of man,—
Inquisitor! incognizable Word
Of Eden and the enchained Sepulchre,
Into thy steep savannahs, burning blue,
Utter to loneliness the sail is true.

All that transpires in an individual's life, the whirlpool of breath between birth and death, is a search for the meaning of the enigmatic parable God has drawn in man. That meaning is thought to lie in love, but the search is a cruel one, because the individual's experience seems constantly to threaten that interpretation, and the search must be carried out ultimately alone.

In stanza ten ("Who grindest oar, and urging the mast") this God sounds like the God of *Tamburlaine.* The majesty and scope of the world he has made give an awesome authority to the revelation in which Columbus trusts. And in the next stanza the resources man has for making decisions and guiding his own life seem dangerously weak without that authority. The heavens, though, are witness enough to the power and order of the universe. In the last stanza it is clear that the purpose of God can be seen as immanent in the universe as long as its accomplishment lies concealed in the future. Desire and hope give the world its meaning and beauty. The last invocation, "O Thou Hand of Fire," suggests what the real issue is in Columbus' faith. It is the destructiveness of the world, which Columbus knows intimately on the sea, which must be construed as the unfolding of a Divine plan.

We must try to understand why Crane began *The Bridge,* after the introductory poem, with this ambiguous success of Columbus. The reason is not, I believe, that Columbus' questing spirit and his return from Cathay represent any redemptive effort of Crane's. Columbus' success and his faith are too equivocal to be

Vision of the Voyage

seen in such a simple way. Columbus' point of view is presented first, because his method of coping with experience is the one every person uses most. The way we structure experience is to imagine that a pattern, or *the* pattern, will eventually emerge so that we will be master of the situation. Even strategies of defeat may be interpreted as means to cognitive mastery. What is important to us is knowing where we are, where we have been, and where we are going; and our chief source of this knowledge is the reassurance of an authority we trust. In other words we see in the way Columbus interprets the past, his world, and his own mission how the sense of value is generally structured and protected. Columbus' understanding of his situation is a form of unself-conscious knowledge (like the sea gull's flight or going to the movies) supported by an unquestioned metaphysic. This is the place we always begin in introspection, in the mediation of our own experience.

The glosses which counterpoint the lyrics help to clarify the psychological significance of Columbus' musings on his return voyage. We may interpret the glosses which link "Ave Maria" and "The Harbor Dawn" something like this—More than four hundred years separate your experience from that of Columbus, or does that historical distance matter at all when we consider experience in its waking and dreaming aspects as it emerges from the complete unconsciousness of sleep?—The implication is that perhaps generations of people do not so much progress through history, as emerge over and over again from unconsciousness into consciousness, repeating the same cultural patterns, structuring values in the same ways. "The Harbor Dawn" is set in the twilight realm between sleep and waking when dreams seem real and sights and sounds around us easily become incorporated into the frame of our dreams. Columbus, we may say, has just been pictured in a kind of dream world—the dream of his accomplished mission, of the great future his discovery would make possible for Spain, and of the cosmic scheme in which he feels he plays such an important part. Now "The Harbor Dawn"

The Bridge: *The Meaning of Suffering*

transforms Columbus' situation into that of the sleepy lover, which could occur at any time and place in history.

The first four stanzas capture the fluidity of definition one's experience takes on in this twilight realm. And synesthesia in these beautiful lines has psychological implications. Ordinarily sights and sounds condition each others' apprehension. When one is alert, a sound is quickly recognized and identified by a visual image of what probably produced it. And seeing objects prepares us for the sounds they will make. But the person who is almost asleep lacks the energy to discriminate; the editorial functions of his mind are relaxed. Strictly speaking there is no perceptual faculty for apprehending "gongs in white surplices," but under these conditions the notion of fog easily leads to surplice and fuses with the distant sound of a bell. Consciousness ebbs and flows in this poem. In the second stanza the mind is slightly more awake so the sounds are immediately identified. But in the third stanza the metaphors become tenuous again. And at the end of the fourth stanza the eyes settle languidly on the chair, half-covered with clothes. Acquiescence is characteristic of this frame of mind in which the meaning of reality is seen not as problematical, but as self-evident.

As we saw in "Voyages," this frame of mind is the best for love. And the poet wishes to prolong this twilight period with its protection from the alluring and threatening involvements of the day. The sexual imagery of the italicized stanza suggests a kind of union possible only in the world the poet can inhabit now, a world in which the demands and risks of problem solving have been suspended. And the poet appeals to the darkness to come back and swallow the threatening dawn. "The Harbor Dawn" is an alba, a lament for the coming of dawn and the separation of lovers. But the form has been adopted for uniquely Romantic purposes. It is not a parting from a specific lover which is regretted, but the loss of love itself in the poet's mind.

The poem concludes with the treacherous meanings of day breaking into consciousness. Fog, dreams, a star—these symbols

Vision of the Voyage

are created by the imagination as it makes a place for itself in the world. They are dispersed by a discriminating consciousness, but they always promise to reappear. The glosses should not be taken lightly in this poem. They emphasize the dreamlike character of love, and they introduce the element of doubt as light begins to break through the window. It is significant that the first allusion to Pocahontas in these glosses is in the form of a question. For she, like Helen, is a highly equivocal figure. She is not identified as the beloved; the feet of poet and beloved have moved upon her. And she should not be narrowly interpreted as the land or any mythos of America. She is what one stands on metaphorically in knowledge. Like Helen, she symbolizes the sense of value, which is the always questionable basis for the interpretation of any experience. And with the conclusion of this poem and the breaking in of light upon the processes of the mind, the sense of value comes under scrutiny.

Understood in this way, the characterization of Pocahontas on the title page of "Powhatan's Daughter"[3] is understandable. "Well-featured but wanton," she fascinates the young, making them do cartwheels. Crane's portrayal of Pocahontas is like that of the young girl on the streetcar in "Faustus and Helen." She can be seen as quite ordinary or, in the right frame of mind, as mysterious and wonderful. And she represents for the poet the point of departure for his voyage into his own experience, as he begins to realize what values give his world the shape it has.

The experience presented in "Ave Maria" was, from Columbus' point of view, relatively unself-conscious, unthreatened by awareness of alternative interpretations of it. In "The Harbor Dawn" the poet watches the shape of his own experience change, as it loses and gains definition. And now in "Van Winkle" he regards himself totally as an other, using the second person pronoun. The theme of the poem is similar to that of "My

---

[3]From a review of W. C. Williams' *In the American Grain* (1925) by Kay Boyle in *transition*. Lewis, pp. 288-289.

The Bridge: *The Meaning of Suffering*

Grandmother's Love Letters," the irretrievability of the past and the impossibility of building a present or future continuous with it. To put it another way, value must always be experienced as newly masked. The attempt to master the sense of value by understanding how it operated or failed to operate in the past and thus to make it predictable in the future fails.

There is something deceptive about a long highway like the one in the first and last stanzas of this poem. It seems to link vastly distant places together, when actually it only makes traveling from one to another possible. A person cannot be in both places at once, so neither space nor time is overcome. The highway lacks for Crane the symbolic ambiguity which Brooklyn Bridge held for him. Only negativity is implied by moving along a road from one city to another. It *seems* to conquer space, just as the sound of a hurdy-gurdy seems to carry one back into one's childhood. But memory is even more treacherous than a highway; every day at four o'clock in the afternoon seems the same, although it is not. The poet begins to reminisce in stanza two about how real Pizarro, Cortes, and Rip Van Winkle were to him as a child, or perhaps how real they seem to have been. At that time the distinction between "historical" and "fictional" characters was incidental. After stanza three, the mind makes a leap.

> *And Rip forgot the office hours,*
> *and he forgot the pay;*
> *Van Winkle sweeps a tenement*
> *way down on Avenue A, —*

A comparison occurs to the poet between Rip Van Winkle waking up out of his time and a derelict on Avenue A who, in a sense, is in the same predicament. In his position, he might as well have slept the last twenty years. We speak of someone "waking up too late" when he fails to structure a way of life for himself which could be the basis of a secure future. The next stanza returns to the hurdy-gurdy and memories of childhood, but

Vision of the Voyage

the dilemma of Rip Van Winkle and the derelict is the key to understanding the rest of the poem.

The first memories evoked are those of excitement—stoning the garter snakes and launching the monoplanes—and of danger—the threatening aspects of those snakes. But the other train of thought, about Van Winkle, again breaks in; this time the poet imagines Rip waking up today and trying to orient himself on Broadway with only the memory of a daisy chain. And Crane uses the hopelessness of Rip's situation to measure his attempt at understanding his own past. The antecedent of "it" in the eighth stanza ("So memory, that strikes a rhyme out of a box") is probably "memory," which produces order where there is none and retrieves sensuous facts from the past in a miraculous and suspicious way. So Crane raises the question, are these two experiences, the whipping and the unconscious smile of his mother, only the fictions of memory? He dwells nostalgically on these vivid and haunting memories, but he realizes that, like Rip Van Winkle, they are no longer "here nor there." The present is traveling down that highway. So Crane repeats the first two lines of the poem, suggesting the endless process of negating past experience which constitutes living. And Rip, who now stands for anyone realizing the deceptive character of memory, does all he can do, move ahead.

> Keep hold of that nickel for car-change, Rip,—
> Have you got your *"Times"*—?
> And hurry along, Van Winkle—it's getting late!

The newspaper represents the constant attempt, which must be repeated every day and which is always a failure, to conceptualize the present on the basis of the past or the past on the basis of the present.

The painful nostalgia of "Van Winkle" illustrates the mind's futile desire to escape the dialectical character of thinking. Since every response becomes a stimulus in its own right, the mind seems to be always just beyond its own experience. It longs to go

The Bridge: *The Meaning of Suffering*

back and repeat, hoping to make its own life more substantial. But the phenomenal world mercifully defeats this desire, saving the mind from losing both itself and the world in fantasy. In the glosses Pocahontas is compared to memory. She is "time's truant," the vital yet hazardous longing after meaningfulness.

If one cannot find himself in memories of his own experience, where does he turn? He turns to the world around him, trying to find continuities in nature or in his culture. He would like to locate himself as part of a larger whole. Columbus, we saw, managed to do this well enough. The sea, the stars, the earth, his voyage and accomplishment, all served to identify him in a large meaningful context. He was lucky, but he was also utterly deceived and in a most vulnerable situation. Without Columbus' faith an individual feels less confirmed in his place in the scheme of things. Such an individual, a modern and awakened Rip Van Winkle, a disillusioned Columbus, looks around him and sees the world of "The River."

The pastiche of advertisements, cultural promises and prophecies which opens this section reminds us of the movie screen in "To Brooklyn Bridge." As if traveling across the countryside at high speed, we catch glimpses of things which people temporarily put their trust in or want. Political slogans and clichés are as important in such a survey as religion. These various symbols of value comprise the world in which people such as the passengers on the 20th Century Limited move, for these symbols are occasions for the expression of desire. But Crane is seeking a slightly foreign perspective on these symbols of value, one that casts them in a new and revealing light. So he focuses upon three bums who are not on the train itself but who watch it disappearing in the night.

Crane is interested in these hoboes, because they do not seem to respond like other people to the enticements and threats of civilization. They seem to have evaded the vast network of communication which has covered the country. But Crane avoids sentimentalizing these old men in stanza six ("Behind/My

Vision of the Voyage

father's cannery works I used to see"). He puts them and their values at a remove by remembering how he viewed them when he was younger. He did not see them as Whitman's Travelers of the Open Road, but as men who somehow never grew up, sad old men without wives or commitments to keep them from running away. They could never take themselves or society seriously enough to make permanent attachments. It was always easier to act as though life were a game and take the slow freight to Tallahassee.

But now he considers them again, and they come to represent a certain state of mind which is portrayed in stanza seven ("Yet they touch something like a key perhaps") and the glosses. They represent a state of mind which has access to the power symbolized in Pocahontas. Pocahontas led us over the highway and back through time in "Van Winkle." And she still leads us in "The River" over the rails and into the lives of these hoboes. These men are presented as knowing her body intimately under the aspect of the land. This experience, Crane says, he knows well and can appreciate. The hoboes are men who have nothing left to lose. Having failed at all the ways the passengers on the 20th Century orient themselves, they are content to take life as it comes. The hoboes represent a state of mind which is part of the dialectic Crane is examining. They have abandoned the attempt to control their own lives. So Crane, looking through their eyes at the whole panorama of the poem, sees the oblivion toward which everyone on and off the train is moving. Crane sees through their eyes, although they do not necessarily see, that the abundance of life is a gift that can neither be earned nor possessed for long. In this sense the hoboes "have touched (Pocahontas), knowing her without name."

We understand how the poet uses these figures for his own Romantic purposes in stanza eight ("And past the circuit of the lamp's thin flame"). There Crane is reading at his desk late at night, letting his mind settle on and go beyond the name of Pocahontas. The sound of a train suggests great distances into

The Bridge: *The Meaning of Suffering*

which he must reach to find her, and he seems to hear the sound of the wind as a papoose crying. Then he realizes that these sounds do not really carry the meanings he is associating with them. In other words he uses these sounds and concepts as Romantic symbols, letting them carry profound meaning much as Wordsworth might in thinking about his vagrants; then he focuses upon the symbols merely as remnants of history, empty of that meaning. The effect of "Dead echoes!" in line eight is much like that of the pivotal word "Forlorn" in the last stanza of "Ode to a Nightingale." In both cases we must realize that a symbol is meaningful or meaningless according to the dispensation of the beholder. Crane is completely aware in "The River" of the semiotic aspect of his characters: he makes their meaning self-conscious and thus transparent.

However, he concludes this stanza with a symbolic image which expresses the intuition he was able to reach at his desk after looking through the alienated eyes of the hoboes. His intuition pictures the figure of Pocahontas with a serpent (time) and an eagle (space). These symbols express the mysterious freedom of the sense of value from all categorical definitions, even those of time and space. Both time and space can be experienced only as negation and thus as loss. One is aware of time by getting older and of space by leaving one place after another. Similarly, living as one ordinarily does, in terms of specific values, one accepts the limitations which are imposed as the self achieves definition through its desires. These limitations constitute another kind of loss. But the Romantic experience of value transcends negation and loss through the creation of a symbol which does not define the self in specific cultural terms, but which makes a powerful emotional response possible outside cultural definition. The Romantic experience of value negates negation. So Crane, in the symbols of the serpent and eagle with Pocahontas, is not giving us mere abstractions. He is suggesting an alternative point of view to that of the passengers on the 20th Century Limited. He has found a way to experience and repre-

Vision of the Voyage

sent value without at the same time committing the self to definition and consistently patterned behavior. This experience of value transcends the dilemma Columbus created by his kind of belief.

The glosses help us understand stanza nine ("Under the Ozarks, domed by Iron Mountain") in light of what has gone before. The point is that the hoboes know nothing about the old rain gods which lie buried now and forgotten. But they do not need them. Similarly, as the poet uses the symbols of stanza eight and the perspective he gains by means of the hoboes to free his sense of value from cultural definition, he does not need to believe that these symbols in themselves are anything but "dead echoes." Therefore, we must not make the mistake of believing that Crane is searching for any unifying myth for the American consciousness. Crane uses symbols to express elusive intuitions about how life is lived through and beyond the mind's objectifications of reality.

The image of iron links stanzas nine and ten ("And Pullman breakfasters glide glistening steel"). Iron has killed and buried the old myths and thus stands for the modern world. And iron brings us back to the passengers on the train as it crosses the Mississippi. At this point the destinies of two groups of people, the passengers and the riverboat characters, momentarily intersect. By juxtaposing these two sensibilities Crane is placing the passengers' lives in a larger context than the one defined by the billboards and slogans.

> Oh, lean from the window, if the train slows down,
> As though you touched hands with some ancient
>   clown,
> —A little while gaze absently below
> And hum *Deep River* with them while they go.

He is offering them, as it were, a deep imaginative experience which reveals the mystery of their lives, for which the best metaphor is the river itself. Crane offers this imaginative experi-

The Bridge: *The Meaning of Suffering*

ence to the passengers, speaking in the imperative mood. But at the same time he sees through any hope he raises for the deepening of their lives.

> And few evade full measure of their fate;
> Always they smile out eerily what they seem.
> I could believe he joked at heaven's gate—
> Dan Midland—jolted from the cold brake-beam.

Crane is speaking here about the power held over people by their own appearances. Who or what a person thinks he is determines his fate. And while it is possible to change, few do.

"They" of stanza twelve ("Down, down—born pioneers in time's despite") refers to the people of the preceding stanza and by implication to all men. The conception of man as a pioneer who has nothing to discover invites comparison with Columbus. Whether one is a lost soul or a frontiersman depends on one's own interpretation of his situation. I suggested that Columbus' pioneering spirit was really the fundamental pattern of problem solving. But in this stanza the equivocal nature of that pattern is recognized. Measured against phenomenal reality, goal-directed activity is seen to be a feeble strategy to defeat time by dreaming. And one's individuality in such a light counts for very little. A man and his father and his father's father all repeat the same strategies in slightly differing forms. The river of time carries the anonymous debris of history to the sea.

> The River, spreading, flows—and spends your dream.
> What are you, lost within this tideless spell?
> You are your father's father, and the stream—
> A liquid theme that floating niggers swell.

This is not a flattering picture of man's purposes and accomplishments.

The last five glorious quatrains of "The River" deal with physical aspects of the Mississippi and not metaphoric ones. The poem does not end with a hymn of praise to the land or to the

Vision of the Voyage

river as the body of Pocahontas. We are not left with the deep imaginative experience which the poet used the hoboes to present. The poem ends with a return to phenomenal reality, to the river which will not be tamed or conceptualized, whose only will is to lose itself in the infinite sea. The viability of the imaginative experience Crane is offering the passengers depends on their willingness to see their lives as a process of irredeemable loss. The river is a perfect metaphor to suggest such a vision of life. Its symbolic power lies in its ability to break down any conceptualization it suggests. It is endlessly fascinating in its variety and changefulness, always bigger than our minds. And the same could be said about this section of *The Bridge*. The whole sweep of the poem brings a realization to life as it is ordinarily lived; it strips away the masks which protect us from seeing the destruction we live in the midst of, so that we can appreciate the miraculous recurrence of value and beauty. Such a realization does not end in apocalypse or a revealed truth, but in the continual rediscovery of the phenomenal world.

Again the glosses help us understand the transition between this poem and the next, "The Dance." They comprise a long sentence which begins in "Van Winkle" and which points back, by pronoun antecedent, to the question raised at the end of "The Harbor Dawn." We should be aware, then, that the woman we will meet at last is the mysterious source and end of the lovers' passion in their "waking dream." She has been our guide all along, through the past in "Van Winkle" and through the complex experience of "The River." She has led us toward insights which free the mind to conceive experience in new ways. This woman has led us "to and fro in the earth," stripping away the masks which stabilize our valuational interpretations of experience. In this way we have come to understand the sense of value as a power prior to societal and personal definitions of good and evil: it is stronger and more dangerous than both. We have discovered the ambiguity of the objective world, and of the "self." This education has been one of suffering, for it forces the

The Bridge: *The Meaning of Suffering*

individual to give up, one after another, the cultural values with which he identifies and from which he derives his own sense of worth. But one experiences the external world, or characterizes it, through one's own various identities; therefore, suspending the notion of who one is allows the world to take on new shapes, new meanings. To put it metaphorically, by embracing death one wakes anew to the world. This is the meaning of the phoenix.

And it is also the meaning of "The Dance." The poem is a dramatic symbolization, somewhat in the spirit of "Lachrymae Christi," of what has been learned thus far in *The Bridge*. It is a summing up and differs technically from the earlier lyrics we have examined. Crane's usual poetic method is to push introspection forward by casting immediate experience in a new light, so that its controlling values become transparent. His poems like "The Harbor Dawn," "Van Winkle," and "The River" lead us through complex experiences which educate us, but they do not formulate for use what we should have learned. "The Dance," however, is such a formulation in dramatic-symbolic terms.

What do Maquokeeta and Pocahontas represent in the poem and what is their relationship? Pocahontas is identified in the first stanza with the cycles of nature, not, that is, with phenomenal reality as represented by the river, but with the recognizable patterns in nature with which we must move in rhythm in order to survive.

> She ran the neighing canyons all the spring;
> She spouted arms; she rose with maize—to die.

We might say that she represents meaningfulness in nature, not, however, benevolence. And Maquokeeta, Pocahontas' lover, represents man's continuing effort to discover that meaningful pattern, to move in rhythm with it, and thus to prosper.

> And in the autumn drouth, whose burnished hands
> With mineral wariness found out the stone
> Where prayers, forgotten, streamed the mesa sands?
> He holds the twilight's dim, perpetual throne.

Vision of the Voyage

He seems to have the power to escort in the seasons and bring rain in time of drought. I believe that Crane's fascination with myth lies in its dual power to represent the world and to ritualize our relationship to it. Like Chanticleer, we are easily deceived as to whether we are active or passive in our relationship to the world. We seem to alternate between feeling active, as we give ourselves and our "external" world directions, and passive, as we carry out those directions ourselves, even as we interpret the world in such a way that it *seems* to have carried out our directions. Therefore, it is significant that Crane introduces Pocahontas and Maquokeeta with questions. "Who squired the glacier woman down the sky?"—or did anyone?

In Crane's poetry imaginative control over the world or feelings of intense meaningfulness are often expressed in a state of semidarkness or dream. So Maquokeeta is pictured enthroned in eternal twilight, the "mythical brows" in stanza three that retire before the presence of Pocahontas. So he is also placed, with the whole world of the Indian and myth, in the distant past. It is interesting that the brows are described as "disturbed and destined," for such a description applies to someone questioning his sense of control over an environment which he formerly took for granted. But Pocahontas is presented only as fresh, untouched, and proud, again very much like Helen in "Faustus and Helen I." This contrast is part of the larger differences between these two figures which will be expanded later in the poem. Maquokeeta is identified with the temporary efforts of the mind to know and control the world; Pocahontas is identified with the processes of nature which outlast those attempts.

It is instructive to compare the way the poet knows Pocahontas in stanzas five ("I left the village for dogwood. By the canoe") through ten ("Over how many bluffs, tarns, streams I sped!") with the way Maquokeeta knew her in the first four stanzas. The poet is not concerned with mastering the life processes in nature. Instead he uses her as the occasion for experiencing beauty and value quite apart from any practical purposes. Maquokeeta's

The Bridge: *The Meaning of Suffering*

religious relationship with Pocahontas takes place strictly within the tribal institution; her meaning is a public one, and he is performing an acknowledged societal function in his courtship of her. On the other hand the poet leaves his village in order to find Pocahontas. Her meaning for him is personal and aesthetic. She is the occasion for a stylistic ordering of his perceptions. This ordering can take place only in a protected setting, so he embarks on a canoe trip alone. The imaginative experience described in these stanzas recalls that of "The Harbor Dawn," and we may even say that the star of stanza seven ("And one star, swinging, take its place, alone") is the one we were promised "at some distant hill." But this experience is only a prelude to the most important section of the poem, stanzas eleven ("A distant cloud, a thunder-bud—it grew") and following. The solitary period in which the natural objects seen by the poet free his mind from its habitual definitions prepares for his identification with Maquokeeta in the next section of the poem. We saw a similar psychological process dramatized in "The Wine Menagerie." There intoxication and the metaphoric reinterpretation of the bottles on the bar and the sound of a drink being poured prepared for the poet's identification with the couple he saw at the table. Similarly the poet now prepares to give up his own role identifications in order to become Maquokeeta temporarily, to enter into his dance and sacrifice.

The description of what follows is highly ambiguous. It seems to be a thunderstorm transformed into a ritual sacrifice. The sound of thunder in the clouds is identified with the rhythmic pounding of feet around a stake, until something emotionally stagnant within the poet is purged. I read the line "Siphoned the black pool from the heart's hot root!" as the final giving over of personal identity to this imaginative experience. It is as if the passions in their efforts to subdue the world accumulate some rancid liquid which must from time to time be drawn off in total forgetfulness. The poet appears to join in the dance around the bound chief, urging him to accept death. Then all of nature enters the ceremony, and the storm is known to be the grieving Pocahontas.

In stanzas fifteen ("Dance, Maquokeeta! snake that lives before") and sixteen the poet regains a certain amount of distance from his own experience. As he did in stanzas seven ("New thresholds, new anatomies! Wine talons") and eight of "The Wine Menagerie," Crane conceptualizes what he finds himself doing. And he sees clearly what Maquokeeta means to him as well as what the whole dance actually accomplishes. Maquokeeta is pictured as a snake shedding his old skin and going on to new life. This is an image very much like the phoenix. It symbolizes the necessity of dying to one conceptualization of experience so that a new one may form. Notice, though, that the process by which this transformation occurs is seen as a lie. Crane is not saying that the transformation itself is a deception, but that change requires the mask of illusion. The reader must be careful at this point not to lose sight of the psychological drama being enacted in the novelty of its mythical setting. We see here the way the mind conceives itself within an institution and the way it loses an old self-conception in order to become something else. Crane uses the Indian mythical setting because it provides a symbology for discussing institutions in general and at the same time sustains his alienation. He can join in these ceremonies only imaginatively, so he can also easily make this experience self-conscious.

The poet endures, as if he were Maquokeeta, the agony of change. But he is more than Maquokeeta, who does not understand the process he himself is undergoing at the time. The poet has left one institution (the village) in order to observe institutional behavior in general. The death-dance of Maquokeeta is really an enactment of something the poet himself has been through, but now in a form in which he can achieve distance and self-awareness. We must be sure to understand the character of the poet's agony during this experience. The sustaining illusion of every effort to cope with the phenomenal world (the effort

The Bridge: *The Meaning of Suffering*

represented in the figure of Maquokeeta) is the stability of selfhood. The self must see itself as stable while it "manipulates" the world. But what the poet must now realize as he observes himself die under the aspect of Maquokeeta is that the sense of control over the world is only a function of enforcing a style of perceiving that world. Maquokeeta's death is represented in terms of an assault by the destructive aspects of the world: lava, stag's teeth, flame cataracts. As in "Lachrymae Christi" the point is not that nature is vicious, but that destruction is a major aspect of becoming. Embracing that aspect of existence frees the individual to penetrate the illusion of control he has over his environment without at the same time feeling himself to be the pawn of "forces" beyond himself.

The vagueness of reference in the long prepositional phrase which introduces stanza nineteen ("O, like the lizard in the furious noon") is significant. One feels that it should modify Maquokeeta or at least "thy change," but it must modify "I." At this point the poet is able not only to accept his identification with Maquokeeta, but also to recharacterize his attitude toward that identification. The last two stanzas before the break remind us of "Legend" in their imagery and the frame of mind they suggest. The agony of change has been lived through, and the poet's awareness of what he has seen in himself prepares for a new attitude toward loss. Thus stanza nineteen makes two points: that laughter, or a spirit of acceptance and joy, may constitute one's response to change as easily as sorrow, and that the problem of freedom versus determinism is really specious. It is as if the poet and Maquokeeta had at last mastered what is natural to the whole nonhuman world, living without regret in a world of change.

The conclusion of "The Dance" suggests that the effort to possess and control the world is founded on self-deception. The sacrifice of Maquokeeta represents the process within institutionalized behavior whereby one pattern of conceptualized experience is given up in a publicly justified way so that a new role may

Vision of the Voyage

be taken on. But at this point the poem is difficult and subtle. No younger chief replaces Maquokeeta. No new role is formed. Instead, the transfigured soul of the Indian chief is presented as having achieved new freedom and insight. He looks out across history at all conquests and the dead, seeing his bride immortal in the renewing processes of nature. Like Faustus he grasps the paradox that to possess the world is to lose it. The richness and beauty (Pocahontas' "largesse") of experience depends on his willingness to let go of it in one form, so that it may reappear in new forms. His transfiguration beyond the human sphere represents for the poet the transcendence of role-playing. Thus Pocahontas is characterized as an eternal virgin. And her reality evades final definition. Notice in the next to last stanza that questions reappear. We might say that a renewed perspective on the world results in wonderment and inquisitiveness.

The dance referred to in the title is both of life and death: it represents all the patterns in and beyond ourselves through which life is destroyed and renewed. The poem dramatizes the poet's efforts to enter that dance with self-awareness. In order to do so, he must penetrate two sets of masks. The first is the illusion of control one seems to have over the external world. Thus Maquokeeta is first presented as active in his sacramental courtship of Pocahontas. But by the end of the poem he has surrendered his effort to know and control nature. Under institutional sanction (the Medicine-man's lie) he is able to accept his own destruction by the forces he previously sought to control. In this way, he comes to see nature as abundant but unconservable. The word for Pocahontas, like Helen, is "prodigal," meaning both "yielding abundantly" and "wasteful." The second mask is that of institutionalization, the control of responses through policed role identification. It is the sense of individuation and consistency that the poet is able to defeat in his identification with Maquokeeta's sacrifice.

The last manifestation of Pocahontas is in the "mother's farewell gaze" of "Indiana." We return now to the psychology of

The Bridge: *The Meaning of Suffering*

everyday life. Why does Crane close this section of *The Bridge* with a poem about the meaning a woman assigns her son's final departure? One of the most endearing habits of Crane's way of thinking is his return, after a devastating introspective analysis of values and motivations, to the simple, incontestable feelings with which he began. We saw this pattern in "The Fernery" and it contributes to the charm of "Chaplinesque." Now after the most difficult poem in *The Bridge* we find the most self-effacing. Underlying "Indiana" is the question posed throughout "Powhatan's Daughter": what leads us through the violent spending of our lives? Crane explores the question now through the psychology of the mother, in her recollections of her family's troubles and in her affirmation at her son's departure. Her memories recall her youthful dreams. She and her husband Jim had given up one way of life in hopes of finding wealth in the gold rush. In her characterization of this dream of Eldorado, we glimpse something of the meaning her dream held. Like Columbus' Cathay, it was to have been a solution; but, of course, it only led to new problems. Their experience in traveling west, she says, was an education in the character of God, who proved to be "passing sly." Jim died and was buried on the trail, so the mother with her infant son turned back. She is relating this story to her son so he can perhaps understand the spirit in which she can say goodbye to him. Her affirmative (but not optimistic) frame of mind is possible because of the reinterpretation of her experience after the total failure of her dream.

We can find no better example of the "negation of the negation" than in her reinterpretation. Old values are given up so that more encompassing ones can take their place. Every value the mother had held was defeated by the time of her turning back. And unlike Job and Columbus, she had no unquestionable value to sustain her. So her triumph had to take place *through* loss, not in spite of it. She experiences a moment of empathy with a homeless squaw and, not being able to speak to each other, the two women hold up their infants. Empathy is usually considered

Vision of the Voyage

to be a form of understanding. But it is also a liberation from narrow expectations about what life should deliver. It is a way of appreciating what different forms the sense of value can take. The mother in "Indiana" is freed from despair, much as Wordsworth is by the old leech-gatherer in "Resolution and Independence." She is freed from hope and thus from hopelessness as well.

As I suggested earlier, we ordinarily tend to assume the orientation of rational optimism in problem solving. But if a loss threatens to destroy us, we may entertain the Romantic possibility of embracing pessimism, hoping to transcend it. Of course, there is almost always an alternative to the Romantic position, even if insanity, as we see in Wordsworth's mad vagrants. But this woman does take the Romantic way. By empathizing with the homeless squaw, she forgets her own disappointments for a while and recognizes that the very human condition is a series of irremediable losses. We may apply the Hegelian concept *aufheben* to her behavior, for she negates those losses which threatened her and holds up (literally) her new manifestation of value, her child. I do not believe that this son represents to her one last hope, one last stay against pessimism. For if he did, she could not say goodbye to him at the end of the poem. Indeed the poem's ending proves that she has triumphed *through* loss, for she can accept loss again with no indication that her son will return. That parenthetical "Or will you be a ranger to the end?" is not a mere intensification of sentiment. It suggests the finality of loss which the mother faces now. It makes her affirmation an act of cultural transcendence.

That is not to say, of course, that the mother understands her triumph over circumstances with any detachment, as the poet does, say, in "The Dance." In order for any adjustment to be successful, it must be protected by masks. But we have been trained, so to speak, by the earlier poems in *The Bridge* how to penetrate some of them, so we can appreciate the way she has coped with her experiences. The emotional situation of "Cutty

The Bridge: *The Meaning of Suffering*

Sark," on the other hand, is more complex than that of "Indiana." As in "The Wine Menagerie" we find the poet in a bar allowing the sights and sounds to organize themselves under intoxication into fascinating patterns, then to disintegrate. We also find him talking to an old sailor, addled and drunk, whose half-coherent conversation reveals his way of thinking to be no more stable than the poet's. The poem creates impressions similar to the ebb and flow of consciousness in "The Harbor Dawn," and to the stylistic structuring and restructuring in "The Wine Menagerie" with its emotional violence which keeps coming to the surface and repelling the poet from social involvement. I see no reason for believing that "Cutty Sark" is the beginning of a picture of a parodic and debased modern culture after the unifying vision of what has preceded it. There is no substantive vision in *The Bridge*. The phenomenological examination of value in its many and deceiving forms always begins and ends with immediate experience; no final interpretation justifies or condemns it.

"Cutty Sark" begins with the poet's immediate surface perceptions of the sailor. Crane focuses first upon the reflection of green light from the bar in his glasses, and then upon the absent-minded way his eyes seem to miss what they look at. The poet is enjoying the sailor's appearance in the same way he is listening to the song from the player piano. The reference to Plato implies beauty and order in the organization of ideas which Crane and the sailor at least seem to be sharing. Then through the sailor's conversation we begin to gain insight into his psychology as we did into the mother's in "Indiana." Like Melville's Captain Ahab, this sailor has been deranged by some experience. He was not able to endure, as Columbus was, the mental strain of being at sea too long. The vast arctic waste has killed his sense of time. He can no longer even find his way on board ship, much less keep his watch. Whether he is really an incapacitated sailor or a crazy drunk, he is to Crane a victim of the tenuousness with which the mind grasps reality through its sense of time. The drunk sailor

Vision of the Voyage

knows that his life has disintegrated, but he can do nothing to reorient himself. When he breaks out with "O life's a geyser . . . I can't live on land—!" he is not affirming any love for the sea, but admitting his inability to cope with ordinary problems of any kind. At first Crane sees in the sailor's eyes what he imagines to be adventurous, far-off frontiers, but then he reinterprets those eyes as containing only vacancy and panic. The last we see of the sailor, he is nearly run over by a truck as he stumbles up the street at dawn. Once again light brings with it the harsh and dangerous phenomenal world which will not respect illusions.

As Crane and the sailor sit talking in the bar a song on the player-piano continues to be heard. But it is never heard quite correctly; as the chorus recurs, it is augmented and changed by fluid verbal associations. What the sailor says seems to affect the way Crane hears the song, until in stanza ten ("I saw the frontiers gleaming of his mind") "Atlantis Rose" becomes a "star . . . burning in a gulf of tears." At this point the poet realizes that the song had stopped playing long ago. It has only been ringing in his mind with variations composed by his association with the sailor. Crane has seen through the sailor's hysterical enthusiasm and his own aesthetic fiction about the sailor's adventurous life. This process of unmasking, presented dramatically in the first half of the poem, becomes a comment on time. I suggested earlier that time, considered experientially, means little more than variability of response. We are aware that time has passed only to the extent that we notice differences in our own responses. The sense of control over the self and the world depends on structuring responses in such a way that they are confirmed by the "external world." This is precisely what the sailor is incapable of doing. He thus becomes to Crane a revelation of the vulnerability of the mask of time.

The poet is still drunk when he leaves the bar. As he walks home across Brooklyn Bridge he lets his mind play on some sea-fantasies which occurred to him while the sailor talked. This medley of exciting phrases about journeys and sea-lore culminates in the

The Bridge: *The Meaning of Suffering*

highly ambiguous line "Perennial-*Cutty*-trophied-*Sark!*" It implies that this clipper ship can be placed not only in the context of "gleaming frontiers," but also in the context of drunken conversation. The poet's exciting daydreams about old navies give way to sentimental questions about the whereabouts of adventurers of the past. But as the poet considers these delightful speculations, their implications suddenly become very serious. At first the names of these old ships engage our interest only on the level of the poem from which the epigraph for "Cutty Sark" was taken, Melville's "The Temeraire."[4] Then, however, the questions and spacings of the last lines, together with the puns, make us reinterpret the loss of these ships on the level of Crane's "At Melville's Tomb." These old ships and their sailors really are gone forever, but that thought soon loses its sentimental appeal. In the same way, the sailor in the earlier section of the poem is a delightful old yarn-spinner until we see how nearly he has approached the end of his own world. So the epigraph from Melville on the title page of "Cutty Sark," like the one from Job, contains a dimension of irony, perhaps even of bitter understatement. It suggests that all things pass away and that if we could realize that fact our hold on reality would suddenly feel as tenuous as it really is. The poem also suggests that intoxication in one form or another makes life endurable by diverting us from the answers to the questions we ask.

Crane's epigraphs take on additional implications when viewed in light of their original contexts. It is helpful to remember, in discussing the quote from Whitman on the title page of "Cape Hatteras," that section eight of "Passage to India,"[5] from which these lines come, is about aspiration, not accomplishment. Here Whitman is treating one of the central problems of Romantic psychology. Having given up traditional moral interpretations of

---

[4]Herman Melville, *Collected Poems,* ed. Howard P. Vincent (Chicago: Packard, 1947), p. 37.

[5]Walt Whitman, *Complete Poetry and Selected Prose,* ed. James E. Miller, Jr. (Cambridge: Houghton Mifflin, 1959), p. 293.

Vision of the Voyage

experience, Whitman pictures himself launching out in a mysterious world toward a mysterious God; in stanza six ("Swiftly I shrivel at the thought of God") he says he is terrified. What sustains him? It is the undefined sense of value which he identifies as his Soul, his Self prior to his various social roles. This separable part of him—he speaks to it as a companion—can accept all of life and even smile content at death. It is greater than any force in the world, and Whitman believes that when life is finished and the Soul meets God, this meeting will be like a younger brother melting in the arms of his new found older brother. Here is that nineteenth-century concept of God, not as judge and deliverer, but as the absolute toward which the mind moves as it accepts indeterminate change. But the most interesting point about this section of "Passage to India" is that what strengthens the poet, allowing him to face all the horrors of existence and death, is not God but his own Soul. And the richness of life is not located in that final destination but in the ceaseless exploration which precedes it. Indeed the focus of Whitman's whole poem is upon voyaging into the unknown, not upon arriving somewhere.

Why, then, does Crane take the lines of his epigraph from the last stanza of section eight of "Passage to India"? Out of context the quote seems to be saying the same thing as the epigraph from Seneca for "Ave Maria." But the earlier quote looks forward to the time when man will become, in effect, master of the globe. This vision justifies Columbus' efforts, as we have seen, although Crane undercuts it with dramatic irony. The epigraph for "Cape Hatteras," on the other hand, points toward a very different consummation—it is simply the end of life joyfully accepted. As we shall see, Crane honored Whitman in the role of wound-dresser, just as Allen Ginsberg did later when he called Whitman "lonely old courage teacher."[6] And the quote on the

---

[6] Allen Ginsberg, "A Supermarket in California" in *Howl and Other Poems* (San Francisco: City Lights Books, 1956), p. 23.

The Bridge: *The Meaning of Suffering*

title page of this poem points to the greatest strength Whitman marshalled, the strength to face the end of life with peace and with love for his own soul above all else. As "Passage to India" suggests, this strength is the ability to refurbish one's emotional life by continual self-transcendence. Like Crane's "Recitative" and other poems in which he addresses himself in the second person, "Passage to India" demonstrates how one renews his relationship to the world by dissociating himself from previous self-conceptions. This process of renewal is central to Crane's vision, so he identifies the spirit of Whitman with the Bridge itself.

> Our Meistersinger, thou set breath in steel;
> And it was thou who on the boldest heel
> Stood up and flung the span on even wing
> Of that great Bridge, our Myth, whereof I sing!

The poem begins with a description of Cape Hatteras from the perspective of a boat. As in "Voyages II" ("adagios of islands") the movement of the boat is attributed to the Cape itself as it seems to rise and sink in the ocean. The associations of the Cape and the land to the west do not serve to particularize or locate this scene geographically, but to universalize it. Land in general is here characterized in somewhat the same way as the River was. Its vastness and timelessness promise to outlast man, and it actually preys on death rather than being defeated by it. The individual is capable of grasping only fleeting perspectives of the land. The poet sees himself traveling all over the globe half understanding the mysterious message of the ocean and of the eternal stars. Finally he returns to the protection of home where his experiences are only vaguely remembered, and the eccentricities he has noticed continue to catch his fancy.

Then the poet's mind turns to Walt Whitman, who represents for him at this point the wandering poet who finds something of deep interest in everything he surveys.

> Or to read you, Walt,—knowing us in thrall

Vision of the Voyage

> To that deep wonderment, our native clay
> Whose depth of red, eternal flesh of Pocahontas—
> Those continental folded aeons, surcharged
> With sweetness below derricks, chimneys, tunnels—
> Is veined by all that time has really pledged us . . .

The source of this wonderment is again personified in the character of Pocahontas. But considering what of lasting value resides in the land leads to the question posed by implication in the second stanza. The flesh of Pocahontas is described as veined by "all that time has really pledged us . . . " Since the flesh of Pocahontas is, metaphorically, the land, veins suggest rivers. And what we recall of the characterization of the Mississippi in "The River" combines with that disturbing "really" to make us wonder what indeed does last through time which makes a positive, assertive vision such as Whitman's possible.

The question is further explored in the next lines through the problem of the present's relation to the past and future. We seem to think, Crane suggests, that modern triumphs over space—the radio and the airplane—represent real progress of some sort. But actually the metaphor of man-at-sea still remains the truest interpretation of man's place in the world. For the limitations and dangers of conceptualization continue to circumscribe his existence no matter what he creates. Therefore time is considered experientially and exclusively from the point of view of the individual's interests. When one considers his joys and pains, he realizes first that they are conditioned by his quite narrow and subjective view of things and then that the way this view has been shaped is through his interpreted past.

> While time clears
> Our lenses, lifts a focus, resurrects
> A periscope to glimpse what joys or pain
> Our eyes can share or answer—then deflects
> Us, shunting to a labyrinth submersed
> Where each sees only his dim past reversed . . .

It is as if he were looking through a telescope into the future

The Bridge: *The Meaning of Suffering*

where he sees only his own past, but reversed, birth reappearing now as death. The point is that one's interests which have exerted themselves through self-definition in the interpretation of the past continue to dominate one's reception of the present moment.

The third stanza ("But that star-glistered salver of infinity") continues this line of speculation, becoming increasingly pessimistic as the theme of war is foreshadowed. The consideration of time from the point of view of experience makes the poet ask what meaning time can have for the whole world: what is infinity? The figure of the circle at the beginning of this stanza suggests the elusiveness of infinity and its immunity to the interests of man.

> But that star-glistered salver of infinity,
> The circle, blind crucible of endless space,
> Is sluiced by motion,—subjugated never.
> Adam and Adam's answer in the forest
> Left Hesperus mirrored in the lucid pool.

When Adam became mortal he had to leave infinity behind him. But it continues to taunt him like the morning (and evening) star shining deceptively in a clear pool of water, as if he could reach out and take it. Now man attempts to conquer space, to impose his will on existence by war. But it is again argued that such a victory is really only an aesthetic one: fact (the phenomenal world) can be grasped only as it is integrated into some dream or plan which produces action.

> Dream cancels dream in this new realm of fact
> From which we wake into the dream of act;
> Seeing himself an atom in a shroud—
> Man hears himself an engine in a cloud!

The reflexive verbs at the end of this stanza are hauntingly Hegelian. They really mean "creates himself as."

The dramatic method of the poem is to alternate pessimistic interpretations of man's attempts to master his world with Whitman's reassurance. That is not to say "Whitman's optimism," for

Vision of the Voyage

it becomes clear in the fourth stanza (" 'Recorders ages hence' —ah, syllables of faith!'') that Whitman's strength, like the mother's of "Indiana," is the result of facing the world on its own terms. This stanza begins with a reference to one of the "Calamus" poems.[7] "Recorders ages hence" is Whitman's address to his readers of the future, in which he tells them that he would like to be remembered as "the tenderest lover," as one who loved passionately and who felt deeply the indifference or absence of his beloved. Whitman's willingness to see the world as inherently valuable and to fully experience its loss represented to Crane the kind of courage required to celebrate life. The fourth stanza is a dialogue with Whitman. Crane recalls the Calamus poems and "Out of the Cradle Endlessly Rocking," asking if his predicament and the older poet's are analogous, if infinity was as attractive and as elusive in Whitman's day as it is now. The answer implied is yes. Whitman's eyes seem to meet Crane's at various points in the modern world.

> Not this our empire yet, but labyrinth
> Wherein your eyes, like the Great Navigator's without ship,
> Gleam from the great stones of each prison crypt
> Of canyoned traffic . . . Confronting the Exchange,
> Surviving in a world of stocks,—they also range
> Across the hills where second timber strays
> Back over Connecticut farms, abandoned pastures,—
> Sea eyes and tidal, undenying, bright with myth!

But the last line suggests that the reason for their kinship is a common understanding of the basic psychological problems shared by all men, problems described in the metaphor man-at-sea in stanza two.

In stanza five ("The nasal whine of power whips a new universe"), however, Crane begins the swing back toward the question of what man has made of man. Here Crane's point is that

[7]Whitman, p. 89.

The Bridge: *The Meaning of Suffering*

the intoxicating glamour of an expression of power blinds people to what is actually transpiring. The new universe of this stanza is not the renewed experience of the phenomenal world, but a new dream, a self-flattering illusion of control over the world. The stylistic experiments of the poetry become extravagant at this point and almost parodic. The attempt to master reality has spun itself into elaborate and impressive patterns which are mistaken by many for a real victory.

A short history of man's fascination with "subjugating infinity" follows in stanza six ("Stars scribble on our eyes the frosty sagas"), beginning with the adventure at Kitty Hawk. Like Columbus, letting his imagination accomplish peace for Spain, the aviator sees Mars within his grasp. "Cape Hatteras," though, carries this kind of imaginative mushrooming one step farther than "Ave Maria." For here it actually ends in self-destruction. Out of the Wright brothers' success has come aerial warfare. "Dragon's covey" points back to the description of the Cape as a dinosaur in stanza one. It is as if a squadron of bombers, bright now with a myth of their own, returned to Cape Hatteras from which they had aboriginally sprung to wreak havoc. This stanza also emphasizes the rationale which accompanies the destruction. "Iliads," "masked," and "theorems" imply an elegant self-deception in the concept of heroism.

From the point of view of someone on the ground, planes in the sky, stars, and clouds share now the same status. Not only has man challenged previously inaccessible regions of the sky, subduing them in a sense, but he has redefined them by his new presence among them on an equal footing. The Pleiades and an Escadrille are now "meaningful" in the same way. Perhaps two analogies from earlier poems in *The Bridge* will clarify what Crane is doing at this point. Columbus, when he is sailing back from what he thinks is Cathay, believes he has achieved a kind of mastery over the elements and over the future. And Maquokeeta, when he thinks he is ushering in the seasons and restoring the land by finding water, also enjoys the illusion of active control

Vision of the Voyage

over the phenomenal world. It is interesting that in both those cases, and in "Cape Hatteras," this sense of mastery is described in terms of the sky. Rather than understanding his situation in terms of the metaphor man-at-sea, Columbus conceives his mission in the eleventh stanza ("Of all that amplitude that time explores") as part of the eternal movement of the stars. And Maquokeeta also sees the patterns of nature which govern all life manifested in the sky. These three dramatic situations suggest that there is a dangerous tendency in any aspiration to conceive one's actions on the basis of a flattering metaphor. The gratification of doing so results from the predictability experience takes on. In the cases of Columbus, Maquokeeta, and the bombers, their styles of performance become vehicles for the sense of value.

The power of style was shown, recall, in "Faustus and Helen III," and Crane's understanding of its power leads him to offer a warning in stanza nine of "Cape Hatteras."

> Thine eyes bicarbonated white by speed, O Skygak, see
> How from thy path above the levin's lance
> Thou sowest doom thou hast nor time nor chance
> To reckon—as thy stilly eyes partake
> What alcohol of space . . . ! Remember, Falcon-Ace,
> Thou hast there in thy wrist a Sanskrit charge
> To conjugate infinity's dim marge—
> Anew . . . !

Here every object of war is stylized. Our mind plays on "turrets," "griffons," "conch of thunder," "searchlights, like/ fencers," until we remember what is actually being described. We are for a while made to be as blind as the Skygak to what is transpiring, because the style of perceiving these actions is so intoxicating in itself. But this stanza ends with a famous admonition, which points the Falcon-Ace back toward the different kind of aspiration we saw in the eighth section of "Passage to India." The rest of "Cape Hatteras" may be read as a clarification of this

The Bridge: *The Meaning of Suffering*

warning—it is what Crane learned from Walt Whitman. Notice, though, that Crane immediately qualifies his words by saying, in effect, that before they can be understood the experience described in stanza ten ("But first, here at this height receive") must be faced.

That experience is unredeemed destruction, pictured as the crash of an airplane. The "shell" of line two points back to "a conch of thunder" in the preceding stanza and reminds us of a similar figure in "At Melville's Tomb." It may also help to bear in mind the sixth stanza of "Lachrymae Christi" ("Let sphinxes from the ripe") which makes the same point as the stanza we are discussing. That is, grasping the imminent reality of death transforms the way one sees the world and makes a new freedom of conceptualization and of action possible.

> But first, here at this height receive
> The benediction of the shell's deep, sure reprieve!

Thus it becomes a blessing, as line two suggests, to undergo a terrifying experience which frees the mind from its illusion of security. The last line of this stanza makes sadly clear that values themselves lead to such an experience of "blessing and dismay."

> By Hatteras bunched the beached heap of high
> bravery!

Now, when pessimism has gone as far as it can go, Whitman is introduced again, and we begin to see what that "Sanskrit charge" means. In stanza eleven ("The stars have grooved our eyes with old persuasions") the stars are associated with victimizing values, and we are reminded of all the promises and prophesies that take man's fancy in the movie theater of "To Brooklyn Bridge" and on the train of "The River." Whitman represents the man who can see through them and still affirm the richness of life because of the strength of his own soul. We may understand the Sanskrit charge, then, to be the responsibility of transcending one's own values. And the psychology Crane recognizes in Whitman's poetry whereby pessimism is confronted and stared down is the route to this transcendence. Notice that the need to go beyond the unquestioning pursuit of one's values is placed in the wrist, in the pulsing blood. Life itself depends on it. And it is not infinity which is conjugated (symbolized in words of various forms), but the dim margin of infinity. Values can be objectified only in the shadow world of self-deception. Still they have to be constantly tested by reality, or we stand in danger of being destroyed by them. The testing process involves forcing ourselves to see the world pessimistically.

As Crane's celebration of Whitman affirms, our greatest hope lies in our ability to question our own values and to create new ones. In the last section of "Cape Hatteras" Whitman is constantly presented as facing the dissolution of things, symbolized by the death of an albatross and those slain in war. Yet he is also presented as traveling forward, searching out new regions. And Crane, after Whitman's example, pictures himself traveling across the countryside seeing nature as revitalized and beautiful. The last stanzas are perhaps the greatest tribute to Whitman ever written. He is apostrophized as Loaf of the Angels, "Our Meistersinger," and as the original conceiver of Crane's central symbol, the Bridge. Whitman's value-bestowing, yet always elusive, mind embodies the same paradox which Crane saw symbolized in the Brooklyn Bridge. And Whitman's eyes are described as a lover's staring into those of his beloved and finding there new riches. The lines about death in stanza fifteen ("Years of the Modern! . . .") refer, I believe, to the famous line from section six of "Song of Myself," "To die is different from what any one supposed, and luckier."[8] And the first line of that stanza, from Whitman's "Years of the Modern!,"[9] continues the dialogue begun earlier by the question "if infinity be the same." All that Whitman prophesied in that poem has come true, and his vision

[8]Ibid., p. 29.
[9]Ibid., p. 339.

The Bridge: *The Meaning of Suffering*

of changes through the years rushing over him like so many dreams acquires for Crane a special poignancy and heroism in retrospect.

The conclusion of "Cape Hatteras" is the happiest moment of *The Bridge*. It may be said to look back and interpret all the lyrics we have discussed thus far, beginning even with the epigraph on the title page. We have learned by this point in the poem to appreciate the character of Romantic suffering. There is no place in it for spiritual or intellectual sanctuary. Neither Whitman nor Crane grants himself amnesty from values; as we have seen, alienation itself results in a kind of victimization. So the suffering which Crane dramatizes in various forms results from discovering repeatedly—with equal pain each time, for one constantly forgets—that the "meaningful" world has been constructed by motives which, in themselves, are only temporarily valuable and perhaps ultimately destructive. The lyrics of *The Bridge* teach the discipline of discovering this paradox. And "Cape Hatteras" teaches how to live with that continuing discovery, without capitulating to despair and withdrawal. Crane emphasizes Whitman's view of himself as passionate and vulnerable lover as well as alien and wound-dresser, because the willingness to engage with the world unironically, to risk oneself, is the first step toward that terrifying yet vitalizing discovery of the meaning of suffering.

It should not be surprising, then, after this hymn to Whitman, to find Crane confronting immediate experience again, beginning with simple, passionate emotions, questioning the world they order for him. I do not believe, as some have suggested,[10] that the poems between "Cape Hatteras" and "Atlantis" represent simply an indictment of Crane's America or of "false values" in general. It should be clear now that the concept of a "false value" as opposed to a "true value" is entirely a device of pre-Romantic thinking; that the distinction merely restates the good-against-evil

---

[10]See Lewis, p. 338 ff.; Dembo, p. 107; and Quinn, p. 94 ff.

Vision of the Voyage

dilemma of Job and does not express the character of Crane's suffering. Similarly, what Crane learned from Whitman was not "the truth" which his poetry now attempts to convey to his readers. He learned from Whitman how to confront suffering and not be overcome by it, so that his own relentless inquiry into the darkest aspects of experience could be carried on.

The epigraph on the title page of "Three Songs" is from Marlowe's unfinished *Hero and Leander*. It represents another instance in which the pursuit of a valued object results in the destruction of the pursuer. And the picture brought to mind of Leander drowning as he tries to reach Hero by swimming the Hellespont also recalls the basic dramatic situation of man-at-sea. The epigraph itself, "The one Sestos, the other Abydos hight," focuses however upon the distance between the two lovers and thus upon the difficulty of their accomplishing in fact what is in their minds. This situation recalls "The Harbor Dawn," which treated the dream-character of erotic involvement and the threat represented to it by the harsh and demanding light of day. And it recalls, of course, the "Voyages" sequence, in which death was first required of the lover—his identity was surrendered as his world became a metaphoric extension of his beloved—and then of the love relationship, as the lover's identity reasserted itself in an attempt to cope with the unsympathetic phenomenal world.

But in "Three Songs" Crane probes into a different aspect of the psychology of love than he does in either of these poems. And his introspection is especially painful at this point in *The Bridge,* just after his celebration of Whitman's love in "Cape Hatteras." Crane presented Whitman's love not as an aesthetic ordering of experience, a victimizing dream, but as a way of engaging passionately with the world, of opening himself, in a sense, to violation. Whitman's poetry is filled with departures and loneliness; he speaks convincingly of the insularity of the individual. But Crane is interested here in exploring the psychological conditions under which that violation takes place.

The scene of Crane's introspection is really, of course, his own

The Bridge: *The Meaning of Suffering*

sensibility. What does he discover that he had expected from love as he faces disappointment? "Southern Cross" begins with a reflection upon a passionate desire in the past: "I wanted you . . . " This seems like a simple enough statement about the pursuit of an unself-conscious value. But the rest of the poem and the next two poems demonstrate what complicated problems underlie those three words. The poet asks himself first what it was he really wanted, and he finds that he cannot define it. He is aboard a ship at night staring up at the Southern Cross, which he uses to personify his passion. And he tries to identify the hypostatized emotional state which is imagined to underlie and support specific emotional involvements. The "nameless Woman of the South" is the powerful, reified goal of Love itself. Crane emphasizes the namelessness of that goal, the difficulty of identifying and locating it. I suggested in discussing "Faustus and Helen I" that the first lines of that poem referred to a tendency people have to reify general impressions, to believe that the most obvious aspects of human behavior represent the terms by which they should measure their personal experiences. Crane is uncovering that tendency with regard to love in "Southern Cross." He is not content to rationalize disappointment; instead, he questions the assumptions behind "wanting" another person romantically.

Eve, Magdalene, and Mary are archetypal women from whom Crane feels estranged. He questions their presence, because they are not as real to him as the "nameless Woman of the South." They are symbols of the collective needs of mankind perfectly answered. But since Crane feels so painfully that these needs are not really met, these symbols appear in the second stanza as grotesque and pathetic. The point of this stanza is not that love since Eve has become debased, but that loneliness may lead an individual to see through his own symbols of happiness.

The poet looks back on the track of waves left by the ship, seeing light playing on the water. And this scene symbolizes for him the way life is lived in time.

Vision of the Voyage

> And this long wake of phosphor,
>   iridescent
> Furrow of all our travel—trailed derision!
> Eyes crumble at its kiss. Its long-drawn spell
> Incites a yell. Slid on that backward vision
> The mind is churned to spittle, whispering hell.

The poet's rediscovery of life through this metaphor casts scorn on his own intellectual pretensions and fills him with terror. For he is deprived of the protection and stability of those symbols of answered needs and their underlying assumption that emotional responses have a universal character. Nevertheless, Crane continues, returning to view his original emotion again, appreciating now the real meaning of his disappointment. He can still recognize the enticement of a generalized conception of love, the "aromatic" quality of the Cross. But the progression in stanza five of blood, fire, and God records the history of introspection which attempts to reconcile erotic experience with any hope to *find* love.

> It is blood to remember; it is fire
> To stammer back . . . It is
> God—your namelessness.

The progression begins with the undeniable facts of physical existence; subjecting life to this degree of honesty destroys its masks like fire; and it ends in an awesome realization—that the namelessness spoken of at the beginning is God. That is, love has stopped meaning an unquestionable spiritual reality which haunts life, making it vaguely disappointing. And in liberating himself from this notion Crane allows his experience a greater freedom in the way it is apprehended. The ultimate expression of this freedom is to define the complete indeterminacy of experience with the highest valuational concept, God.

The conclusion of the poem reminds us of "Lachrymae Christi" with its transformation of a symbolic figure before our eyes. Here the figure becomes a kind of monster. Eve is seen as a

The Bridge: *The Meaning of Suffering*

Medusa rising from the water, and as a ghost from which the poet dissociates himself. By the end of the poem Crane understands that what he had wanted so badly to be real would be an abomination if it were. We may put it this way: if the powerful feelings of devotion, psychological dependency, and desire for possession which characterize "falling in love" were permanently real, if we could not somehow escape or negate them, we would be destroyed by them. But light again obliterates the valued object.

The next of the "Three Songs" is "National Winter Garden," which is a poem about lust. The poet is in a striptease theater observing with detachment the performance of the dancer and his own responses to what he sees. I suggested that one of the liberating discoveries of "Possessions" was that the essence of passion is fantasy, a self-regulating, even if enslaving, repetition of a private emotional syndrome. Crane is pursuing this line of thinking here too: self-consciously watching a striptease show is a way of questioning the psychology of lust. It is an interesting way of separating the experience of sexual fascination from the complex social situation in which it ordinarily takes place. Magdalene represents another overgeneralized conception of experience, the promise of sexual gratification.

The poem begins by emphasizing the frankness with which the sexual object, Magdalene's body, is acknowledged by everyone watching. She is what everyone wants without question. To the audience it is as if the whole world were a potential strip show, but only in the theater is that possibility realized. In the second stanza the poet begins to explore what the audience really does. They know, first of all, that this dance will only awaken their appetites. The gratification of sex, although it is the highest value extolled here, will not actually take place. They are thus protected from measuring this imagined gratification against actual experience. Therefore, although they pick out their favorite blond through the smoke, they do not concentrate their fantasy on her—as they might on a potential prostitute, say—but hurry to

Vision of the Voyage

find another object of desire, another dancer. The element of repetition seems to be more important than the quality of the sexual fantasy. The real gratification is in the predictability responses acquire under these conditions. The hasty exist at the end of the second stanza implies, in addition to some repugnance, the incompleteness of this aggravation of desire.

Stanzas three through six ("We wait that writhing pool") present Crane's disillusionment with the performance. He is aware of the pretense of the dance, the cheapness and artificiality of the passion. Sexual excitement as a cultural value suddenly becomes transparent for him, and he wants to flee this value itself, not merely the theater. But the poem does not end simply with flight. In the last stanza Crane has left the scene of the dance, and he reflects on the power of Magdalene over each separate mind.

> Yet, to the empty trapeze of your flesh,
> O Magdalene, each comes back to die alone.
> Then you, the burlesque of our lust—and faith,
> Lug us back lifeward—bone by infant bone.

He is not talking here about the power of sex purely, but of the set of vague expectations and promises which the striptease artist represents. She is in the minds of her audience as they act out their own individual sexual lives in the real world. In the protected situation of the theater she is an ideal; in light of actual experience she becomes a burlesque of lust. In the setting of the theater she is taken seriously; outside she is only pathetic. But the contradiction between these two interpretations is not recognized by most people. So from the poet's point of view she is also the burlesque of faith in general. Like every cultural value, she seduces and then evaporates. But her deception is what life itself depends upon. The promise of gratification, Crane thus suggests, is what supports action and masks it.

With "Virginia" we turn to the social world in which sexual fascination is acted out. Mary in this poem might seem at first to

The Bridge: *The Meaning of Suffering*

have little in common with Eve and Magdalene of the previous poems. But really she is a combination of both. The picture we have of her reveals how the vulgar notions of love explored in the earlier poems create the clichés of ordinary life. This poem is the most stylized of the three; there is a lovely surface composed of the niceties of courtship and the working girl's psychology of coy survival. But again we have been taught by the earlier poems how to see through this picture. That is not to say it is a cynical poem. Quite the contrary, Crane clearly delights in the glitter of these superficialities in their heavy rhyme and rhythm. Still there are subtle ironies that we cannot miss after reading the other two poems.

We are allowed to see Mary only in a narrow way. She is the Saturday date. But that cliché will not stand up after the general notion of romantic love has been defeated in "Southern Cross." Indeed a comparison between Mary and Eve is suggested in the presentation of both in anachronisms. The picture of a modern Rapunzel in the Woolworth Building is no less incongruous than a contemporary Eve or a "simian Venus." And the last glimpse we get of "Cathedral Mary" in the "nickel-dime tower" pushes generalized appearances into travesty. I do not believe that Crane, in this poem or in the others, is commenting on any uniquely modern vulgarity. He is probing into the vulgarity toward which all thinking tends because it is metaphoric and analogically patterned. The illusions about love with which he has been concerned in these poems comprise the mind he speaks of in "Faustus and Helen I," the mind which is "Too much the baked and labeled dough/Divided by accepted multitudes." Still, it is a mind in which Crane finds beauty and delight. The ironies of "Virginia" are good-natured and humorous.

The last two poems before Crane's return to the central symbol of Brooklyn Bridge face the full implications of the psychological discipline which he has followed thus far. They are a descent into the hell of living such as we have not seen in any of the earlier lyrics. It seems to be Crane's intention to state for himself the

Vision of the Voyage

complete extent of his pessimism. In this way he is able to penetrate perhaps the last mask, the illusion of cognitive mastery in poetry itself. This is the last vestige of redemptionism, the belief that one's knowledge of the illusory nature of thinking exempts one from illusions. Such a belief was central to the Socratic method of argument. As long as the poet feels that his grasp of the psychological dilemmas of man sustains him in a state of spiritual superiority to others, he is still repeating the pattern of Job's thinking. He himself needs another confrontation with the phenomenal world. This, I believe, Crane pursues in "Quaker Hill" and "The Tunnel." Only after he has acknowledged utter hopelessness can he return with honesty to the subject of value in the last poem "Atlantis."

Just such an acknowledgement is suggested in the two epigraphs on the title page of "Quaker Hill." Crane had been powerfully impressed by Isadora Duncan when she danced in Cleveland in 1922.[11] Her famous advice to her unsympathetic audience was to read Whitman, especially the "Calamus" poems. Crane might well have added her words to that effect on the title page of "Cape Hatteras." But it is significant at this point in *The Bridge* that he does not focus upon Duncan's redemptive message, but upon her disillusionment.

> *I see only the ideal. But no ideals have ever been fully successful on this earth.*

It is the hopelessness of the very *raison d'être* of her art that Crane wishes to emphasize. The phrase "fully successful" is, of course, bitterly ironic. The lines of Emily Dickinson are from a poem about the "death" of summer.[12] By imagining nature going

---

[11] See Crane's letter to Gorham Munson, 12 December 1922, *The Letters of Hart Crane,* p. 109.

[12] Emily Dickinson, *The Complete Poems,* ed. Thomas H. Johnson (Boston: Little, Brown and Co., 1960), p. 14.

The Bridge: *The Meaning of Suffering*

through all the pomp that humans go through when they confront dying, she casts a mischievously ironic light over the whole institutional endeavor to explain and justify loss. Dickinson's poem illustrates the preceding quotation from Isadora Duncan. Both epigraphs represent the artist speaking to herself. They are not so much a criticism of society as a personal meditation on futility.

The same may be said for the poem which follows. It is a mistake to read "Quaker Hill" as primarily an indictment of the way of life represented by the New Avalon Hotel. That way of life may or may not be degenerate compared to the one represented by the Quakers in their meeting house. Actually the pathos of the contemporary scene does not result from the poet's preference for the ideals of the Friends. It derives from the disillusionment he reluctantly accepts as he considers the banal efforts of the affluent to sustain themselves in spite of time. Their efforts are even sillier than the funeral Emily Dickinson imagined in the poem mentioned above. The pastimes of the guests are pathetic, not because any other set of values would have served these "Czars/Of golf" better, but because they seem to have carried the universal dilemma of value to its logical but absurd conclusion. Yet they continue oblivious to what they are doing to themselves and to each other.

It is the poet's reaction to his own realization about these people, though, that is most interesting. In the last stanzas he does not withdraw from the scene as he had done in "The Wine Menagerie" and in "National Winter Garden." His understanding of human psychology as vicious exploitation and self-deception does not lead him now to adopt a perspective which implies a purity on his part. He accepts the indictment he must make of human psychology as a personal indictment as well. He accepts the failure of the mind to defeat despair, thus inducing, in "Quaker Hill" and "The Tunnel," the final and most difficult crisis of all.

"Quaker Hill" begins angrily, as if the poet hated so strongly

Vision of the Voyage

the people he is describing that he forgets even to identify them. But by the third stanza we begin to see that he has been talking about vacationers. What he hates most about these resort-dwellers is their nearsightedness, their bovine complacency in their own amusements. They do not seem capable of locating their enthusiasm outside of themselves, even to the extent of recognizing that a change in the seasons might make a new sport possible. Contrasting himself with these inert people, the poet characterizes in the second stanza his own willingness to reach out to others and make himself vulnerable.

> While we who press the cider mill, regarding them—
> We, who with pledges taste the bright annoy
> Of friendship's acid wine, retarding phlegm,
> Shifting reprisals ('til who shall tell us when
> The jest is too sharp to be kindly?) boast
> Much of our store of faith in other men
> Who would, ourselves, stalk down the merriest ghost.

It is significant that Crane introduces at this point the disappointments which necessarily follow emotional commitment—the boredom that creeps in, the subtle slander that becomes a game. For the capacity to feel this kind of pain and, without retaliating, to understand the profound basis for it in human psychology will be pushed to its limits at the end of the poem. The last two lines of the second stanza remind us that Crane championed Whitman's love ethic. Crane seems to be saying that his own good-hearted iconoclasm toward heroes does not stop him from believing in the worth of people in general. He is presenting the kind of personality which could suffer the unmitigated disillusionment of the last stanzas.

In stanzas three and four Crane describes the old hotel in a way the guests would not recognize. For him the hotel is not merely a place to stay when he plays golf, and the view from its central cupola is not that of the three states advertised in some brochure. He begins to think how long the old hotel has stood and what it

The Bridge: *The Meaning of Suffering*

has seen come and go. It has seen more people die than could now inhabit it, and it has seen ideals die as well. The ironies of juxtaposing the "Promised Land" of the old Meeting House with that of the bootlegger and the New Avalon Hotel are chiefly the ironies of seeing values under the aspects of time and change. They make the myopic tourists seem foolish and pitiable and the poet's wounded feelings seem wasted. The point of view of the mouse and of the woodlouse appeal to Crane in this frame of mind. We should pause over that marvellous line beginning stanza six, "What cunning neighbors history has in fine!" Time and various interests of individuals in the present so distort the meaning of the past that events seem to cheat each other out of their significance. The unanswerable rhetorical questions at the end of this stanza suggest, of course, the impossibility of recovering a significance which was problematical to begin with.

It is only the living, not the "resigned factions of the dead" (stanza seven), who are interested in creating a past for their own purposes. This stanza refers mainly to the white man's destruction of Indian culture and to his glorification of what he had done in order to build his own civilization. The "new destiny," part of which led, ironically enough, to the peace-loving Quakers, and then to modern resorts, was made possible only by exploitation and threats.

In the last two stanzas Crane accepts the implications of all that he has been saying for himself. Earlier in the poem there were at least two strongly autobiographical references: to "Shifting reprisals ('til who shall tell us when/The jest is too sharp to be kindly?)" and to the "curse of sundered parentage." And now it is as if the burden of truth were too much for him. Values, I suggested, may be seen as temporary strategies for avoiding the despair which would result from seeing the world as irredeemable. But values actually precede despair, of course, and for most people it is not necessary to interpret them in such a pessimistic way. It *is* necessary for Crane to see them this way at this point in *The Bridge*. Values, throughout the poems and most painfully

Vision of the Voyage

here in "Quaker Hill," have lost for the poet the degree of respectability which makes them function psychologically. It has become impossible, we may say, for Crane to admire anything or even to take his characteristic delight in surfaces. For the dilemma is too serious, too immediate and undeniable. Even his earlier spirit of rage softens into shame, because what he hates in the tourists he must also hate in himself.

> So, must we from the hawk's far stemming view,
> Must we descend as worm's eye to construe
> Our love of all we touch, and take it to the Gate
> As humbly as a guest who knows himself too late,
> His news already told?

Crane induces crisis by seeing the process of individuation itself as pathetically futile and cruel, yet as the very *modus operandi* of the mind and thus as an inescapable condition of living.

The "Gate" of stanza eight points toward the "Gates of Wrath" in the epigraph from Blake for "The Tunnel." In fact, "Quaker Hill" may be read as an introduction to that poem. There is a crucial point as one approaches a pessimistic interpretation of any problem when the mind can turn back and "find" an answer which totally justifies optimism and which restructures the problem on the basis of a metaphysic of unquestioned authority. At that point the hopelessness of seeing one's own values as inextricably caught up in falseness and superficiality seems to demand some immediate and drastic correction. Crane captures this feeling of dread and inadequacy in his figure of the late guest whose news is already told. But the response Crane demands from himself is not a total restructuring of experience, but the attempt to sustain a clear picture of his own hopelessness by singing it metaphorically.

> Yes, while the heart is wrung,
> Arise—yes, take this sheaf of dust upon your tongue!
> In one last angelus lift throbbing throat—
> Listen, transmuting silence with that stilly note

The Bridge: *The Meaning of Suffering*

> Of pain that Emily, that Isadora knew!
> While high from dim elm-chancels hung with dew,
> That triple-noted clause of moonlight—
> Yes, whip-poor-will, unhusks the heart of fright,
> Breaks us and saves, yes, breaks the heart, yet yields
> That patience that is armour and that shields
> Love from despair—when love foresees the end—
> Leaf after autumnal leaf
>   break off,
>   descend—
>   descend—

Crane wants to comprehend the pathos of his own song. And like Emily Dickinson and Isadora Duncan, he recognizes that the only action open to him really is to objectify hopelessness itself. His last assertion of value thus becomes an expression of agony. It is the only perfectly honest response to his own life. What he means when he says that the resulting patience shields love from despair is that the nonmoral values of art make it possible for him to go on in an existence which requires the response of love (or meaningfulness in general) but in which no basis can be found for that response. The expression of suffering unredeemed is the last sublation of experience.

In order to understand "The Tunnel" we must see the full extent of this pessimism. It is one thing to find society or even human psychology lacking by some high standard, but it is another to carry through a program of introspection which completely tears down the personality. And this is what Crane does. This discipline goes beyond indictment and beyond self-hatred, for no alternative is implied to which the mind (as if it were an unbiased judge) may turn. To know oneself is to follow an unending series of revelations of dizzying nausea. There is nothing left to stand on, no reason to avoid seeing the ugliest and most pitiable manifestations of the human will as mirror images of oneself. Indeed the route through pity is suggested by the epigraph from Blake's "Morning." Pity, Crane explained in a

Vision of the Voyage

note in one edition of *The Bridge,* inhabits the West.[13] Since Blake's poem is about daybreak we are led to think that Crane will finally introduce some sort of renewal. But the largest part of "The Tunnel" represents only the suffering that "Quaker Hill" promised.

It is significant that the feeling of narrator identity is so weak in "The Tunnel." The only sustaining value left at this point, that of representing suffering clearly, cannot serve as a basis for any respectable conceptualization of self. One does not create a self-as-other by identifying with the monotonous agonies of living. And unlike every other section of *The Bridge* in which various values are glimpsed quickly, "The Tunnel" does not allow any counteridentity to sustain the poet temporarily. There is no hobo, no Indian, and certainly no Whitman. It is hard to imagine an "interest" strong enough to stabilize any self in the rush of noise and pain that is apprehended with such raw nerves in this poem.

The poet begins speaking in the second person, seeing his own actions and thoughts impersonally, as if they could be anyone's. And the walk from Times Square to Columbus Circle really could be anyone's. Crane uses the sense of anonymity one gets in a crowd on a busy street to shatter the circumscribed and protected sense of self. He also adopts the attitude we saw in "Sunday Morning Apples" of art-perceiver toward what he sees. Billboards and facades become the models for responding to whatever he passes. Having seen these crowds and buildings countless times, he says they are finally memorized; that is, they lose their capacity to surprise him. At the point at which they become stylized, it is as if a curtain lifts on the scenes before him and he sees life as a tedious and repulsive play. The indented second stanza may contain a reference to Christianity.

---

[13]Lewis, p. 355.

The Bridge: *The Meaning of Suffering*

> Then let you reach your hat
> and go.
> As usual, let you—also
> walking down—exclaim
> to twelve upward leaving
> a subscription praise
> for what time slays.

But more generally I understand these lines to mean that one always pays a certain owed respect to whatever meaning seems to have resided in the past. Nothing concerns the poet, however, except getting home and to bed. Confrontation is the last thing he wants, so he would even avoid catching sight of his own eyes reflected in a revolving glass door. His state of mind is dangerously fragile, and the decision in stanza three to take the subway is evidently a mistake.

For in the subway the poet has an experience similar to that on the street but greatly intensified. Here we fully understand what Crane meant in "To Brooklyn Bridge" when he said "Only in darkness is thy shadow clear." For his experience on the subway represents a total immersion in darkness, in which those particulars which seem to distinguish one person's life from another's are obscured. Any bit of conversation overheard or an impression of someone sitting in the car is significant not for the individual it defines but for the general dilemma of man which it symbolizes. What Crane is forced to see and to continue seeing until he gets off the subway is the pathos of being an individual human being. And his last reflection on "some Word that will not die . . . !" in the second to the last stanza is the preparation for reconsidering the meaning of Brooklyn Bridge.

The sameness of voices and faces is like the monotonous motion of the car. Repetition and the loss of individuation (as in the memorized street scene of the first stanza) make the poet begin finding new patterns in the fragments which flash before him. He creates a series of metaphors which temporarily structure the blur of images and words, but which express at the same time the nausea he feels at the hopelessness it all implies. The first is a suggestion in stanza eight (" 'what do you want? getting weak on the links?' ") of an ungratifying sexual encounter. This is followed by an image which captures the darkest themes of "Three Songs."

> The phonographs of hades in the brain
> Are tunnels that re-wind themselves, and love
> A burnt match skating in a urinal—

Then a bit of dialogue ("But I want service in this office SERVICE") recalls the kind of mentality represented by the tourists of "Quaker Hill." The worst kinds of exploitation and victimization which people's desires work on them are briefly recalled. These metaphors are all variations on the theme introduced in the first poem of *The Bridge* by the suicide and the unfeeling crowd.

The "meaning" of the subway ride—the poet's intended destination—has entirely failed to coordinate what he sees and hears. Because he is unable to ignore the suffering and cruelty which are everywhere around him, what he sees and hears breaks down any sense of solidarity in the external world. I suggested that one's sense of the reality of the external world and of the self depends on one's ability to stabilize his own interests. But, as I have tried to show, by this point in *The Bridge* every interest or value the poet finds in others or in himself has been undermined by introspection. Admiration and security have been replaced by nausea and near panic. So no structure seems immanent in the scene before Crane; he has to create a fantasy to make reality meaningful at all. And that fantasy can be only a reiteration of the dilemma of meaninglessness itself.

The next metaphor which construes the images of the subway ride into an expressive fiction is Crane's vision of Poe. This seems to occur to him passively. He cannot at first even recognize this figure in his hallucination. Although he is aware that what he is seeing is not "real," it might as well be. It has for him the same objectivity as the people in the subway car, and he

The Bridge: *The Meaning of Suffering*

questions it as though he himself did not have control over the answers. What Crane sees is a kind of dramatic elaboration upon Poe's alleged murder. It has been pointed out that Poe represented for Crane the Romantic poet destroyed by an unsympathetic public.[14] But Crane's fascination with Poe at this point goes deeper than this. It is first of all the degrading way Poe died that Crane remembers. The psychological and physical violence which is characteristic of human life is exemplified in Crane's vision of the mutilated Poe. The second point to notice about this reference is the focus upon death in the allusions to "The City in the Sea" and "The Raven." Crane associates with Poe the recognition of the finality of loss. This recognition gives the last question in stanza fourteen ("And why do I meet your visage here") its import. It is not simply a question of whether or not Poe maintained his integrity regarding political issues; it is a question of how he faced the death he wrote so much about. The actual demands of his murderers together with the sickening details of his last hours constituted death for him, not an elegantly rhymed poem. So, in effect, Crane is asking Poe if he realized, as Crane himself realizes this moment on the subway, the ugly truth about death in real life. The answer is not important. What is implied by this question is that destruction, as it is truly grasped by the mind, does not so much yield a conceptual understanding of existence as precipitate the dissolution of life as it has been known. The recognition of loss either changes the individual or destroys him.

It is understandable, therefore, that the next stanzas represent the poet regaining some perspective. At this point the subway stops at an exchange, and he begins to see with more coherence. The "Wop washerwoman" reminds us of Columbus and the psychology of his "success." So Crane is remembering that through all the destruction he has witnessed, the genius of man

---

[14]Ibid., p. 359.

Vision of the Voyage

for self-deception in the service of his interests is what makes his life worth the trouble.

> And does the Daemon take you home, also,
> Wop washerwoman, with the bandaged hair?
> After the corridors are swept, the cuspidors—
> The gaunt sky-barracks cleanly now, and bare,
> O Genoese, do you bring mother eyes and hands
> Back home to children and to golden hair?

In this way the subway Daemon, like the River, is the destroyer but also the creator. Stanza eighteen ("Daemon, demurring and eventful yawn!") is a brilliant representation of this paradox.

Crane's acceptance of both the destructive and creative aspects of life without attempting to mitigate either is phrased in such a way that it recalls Columbus' faith and contrasts with it. Crane's prayer "Kiss of our agony Thou gatherest,/O Hand of Fire/ gatherest—" comes out of an acceptance, we might say, both of man's plight at sea and of his starry gaze. Crane's pessimism could not be more complete. Individuals, he says, are "caught like pennies beneath soot and steam," and the most valiant attempts to redeem the world conceptually are no more than "shrill ganglia / Impassioned with some song we fail to keep." Crane is referring here, I believe, to his own poetry. As we saw in his elegy to Ernest Nelson, the clearest evidence of Crane's conviction is his willingness to regard his work, or anyone's, as at best a failure. Yet the figure of Lazarus and the last incarnation reference are, after what has gone before, the most positive assertions so far in the poem.

"The Tunnel" ends with Crane standing by the river thinking of all that has transpired in *The Bridge*. He is looking out over the city much as he was in the first poem, about to consider in "Atlantis" what he began to think about earlier as he puzzled and thrilled over the symbol of the Brooklyn Bridge. By now we appreciate something of what was involved in grasping the paradoxical nature of the life of the mind—forgetting in order to

The Bridge: *The Meaning of Suffering*

conceive—and the unjustifiable cruelty of all life in its continuous creation. The final judgment of teleology is suspended in a hymn of equivocal praise.

It is this sustained ambivalence that we must bear in mind when reading "Atlantis" in order to avoid oversimplifying this poem and all of *The Bridge*. Crane emphasizes that the Bridge is not something to be seen simply as one magnificent structure. Instead it is a complex arrangement of sweeping lines and massive surfaces along which the mind travels back and forth. Although the Bridge is stationary it constantly implies movement, not clearly determined but contingent always on the disposition of the mind exploring it. The same could be said, in a sense, of Crane's poem. All the dramatizations we have seen of aspiration, love, and disappointment were powerfully involving in themselves, but Crane's method has been consistently to mediate these experiences so that no single emotional response appears adequate to explain or justify them. That is, the meaning of each experience remains problematical. As Tate recognized, no moral definition is ever achieved in the poem; it is not a "tragic" work. Rather, the reader is taught how to see the sense of value, which gives the world shape and meaning, as a power which itself uses definitions of good and evil but which is not contained by them.

As I have tried to show, the moral interpretation of experience is one of the means of sustaining the sense of self as opposed to the world. So the suffering which Crane goes through and records in the poem results from seeing the permutations of value in the personality without a structuring goal. Or more correctly, he substitutes the goals of clarity and honesty for those of justification and consistency in the examination of his own experience. Honoring clarity and honesty means to measure one's own responses against the norms which supposedly describe them, but which actually police them. And this, we may say, is what Crane has done in each of the lyrics of *The Bridge*. Like the arching cables that catch the eye and carry it up until it is engaged by other patterns, the various emotions of Columbus, Maquokeeta, the woman of "Indiana," the sailor of "Cutty Sark" are compelling in their own right. But the emotions are all presented in such a way that their vital and sustaining illusions become apparent. Furthermore, Crane applies this same method of analysis to his own most cherished feelings in "Quaker Hill" and "The Tunnel." Grasping how the sense of value has created a world for all his characters in *The Bridge* destroys Crane's own illusions. For he is every character in the poem. Viewing the life situations of others so that they become studies in the psychology we all share is Hegel's method of cultural analysis, and it is Crane's method of poetry. The intense suffering which is central to the poem derives from the realization that, in one sense, every human dilemma is one's own (we can find in the situations of others dramatic elaborations upon our own tendencies) and that, in another sense, the principle of individuation which makes culture and every dilemma possible also condemns us to our own increasingly narrow self-definitions and to their possibly catastrophic results.

"Atlantis" is not an attempt to reconcile man and the world. It does not offer a justification for all the pain we have witnessed as in some way necessary for the accomplishment of a great mission. Rather, this last poem should be read as a celebration of all life, exemplified in the preceding lyrics, with the notion of accomplishment or success suspended. It is thus an insouciant celebration, at the same time joyful and disinterested. The chief artistic problem Crane confronts throughout *The Bridge* is how one defeats the conceptualization of experience—basic goal-directed activity—without merely negating the values of one's immediate culture. His solution is to maintain in the highest esteem a complicated symbol which represents for him at once the myriad aspirations of the human heart and the vast absorbing patterns in which they are eventually lost. Every feature of the Brooklyn Bridge is captivating, yet the eye cannot rest very long on any one single line of it. In this respect it is like the sea,

The Bridge: *The Meaning of Suffering*

always challenging and defeating categorization. But it is a better symbol for Crane's purposes than the sea, for it is a product of culture, deriving from and symbolizing the efforts of the mind to capture reality, to make its own patterns permanent, yet demonstrating at the same time the elusiveness of such goals.

This symbol also poses a tantalizing question about the relationship of the individual to culture. Conceptualization is possible only at the level of the individual; culture itself does not think. Yet only cultural patterns, not individuals, survive. So what man creates, like the Brooklyn Bridge, stands for his power to transcend his own mortality. But at the same time does it witness to the vanity and failure of that endeavor? It should be abundantly clear after reading all of *The Bridge* that deception and pain must be sustained in order for man to impose his will on the world. The Bridge seems to symbolize the indifference of culture to its cost in terms of suffering, or more generally the forgetfulness which must surround every act of "greatness." This is the direction of inquiry with which *The Bridge* concludes—the question of man's glory flung into the face of a silent universe.

"Atlantis," then, does not interpret the rest of the poem for us. It does not tell us how to respond to all we have seen. Rather, it supplies a symbol which, because of its own irresolvable ambiguities, allows the mind to endure the tensions it creates for itself in introspection. There is always a tendency to simplify problems in memory. This is exactly what Crane tries not to do in this last section. To read "Atlantis" with care is to reconsider the basic interpretational problem Crane faced in each of the preceding lyrics: what is one's response to the recognition of the limitations of one's own values? Our ordinary mode of thinking is to structure experience on a paradigm of question-and-answer. We seem to think that these two forms of utterance are in some sense opposites and that when we are able to give an "answer" to a "question" we have achieved a desirable state of equilibrium. But this is a deceptive way of construing experience. Since the only satisfaction for a question is an answer, and since we *must*

Vision of the Voyage

have satisfaction, almost any answer at all will serve our purposes. Questions are asked and answers given which are designed to make that satisfaction easily accessible. Consequently the very *modus operandi* for examining experience, language, becomes only a means of by-passing the important dilemmas, not of confronting them. Within the context of rational optimism our problems become straw men.

This is why it is so important to grasp the centrality of pessimism to the Romantic way of thinking. Only one situation makes us take the notion "problem" seriously: imminent loss or suffering. In such a situation one sees "answers" as facile, and is forced to undergo a really disturbing train of inquiry, one which will not, hopefully, provide him with a new "answer" but which will free him from his own patterns of thought and make it possible for him to change. When one's values stop dictating a catechism which interprets the world, he sees whole new dimensions of his own experience and sees them with a new clarity. The end of *The Bridge* aims at sustaining this clarity by forcing the mind continually to reencounter the phenomenal world. The symbol of the Brooklyn Bridge as the myth lent to God is the instructor of the poet and of the reader in this way of thinking.

Crane compares the Bridge to music. The epigraph from Plato is taken, as well as I can determine, from the *Symposium*,[15] and it needs some clarification. First, we must not make the mistake of reading this epigraph as an endorsement of Plato's idealism and then of expecting "Atlantis" to illustrate it. I discussed above some of Crane's observations about Plato's philosophy which he expressed to Gorham Munson in a letter of 17 March 1926.[16] Crane was able to separate Plato's logic, the elegant design of his

---

[15] Plato, *Symposium, or The Drinking Party*, trans. Michael Joyce in Hamilton and Cairns, p. 540. Joyce translates this passage: "And so we may describe music, too, as a science of love, or of desire—in this case in relation to harmony and rhythm."

[16] *Letters*, pp. 237-240.

The Bridge: *The Meaning of Suffering*

argument, from the meaning of what he said, the power of his philosophy to determine the behavior of his audience. Crane says that Plato lives today because of the former, and that the philosopher himself realized how important it was to protect his style of thinking and arguing from the innovations of poets. Reading the *Laws*,[17] one sees that music may also threaten the sovereignty of argument. For Plato understands music, with its various modes appropriate to different role functions in society, chiefly as a means of policing behavior. It is important that people hear music which reinforces the "right" emotions for their situations and that they not be led by decadent experimenters to indulge dangerously inappropriate feelings. Of course, it is impossible to imagine Crane in sympathy with such a program.

Actually, this line from the *Symposium* is not spoken by Socrates. It is spoken by Eryximachus, a physician, who, called upon to make a speech in praise of love, claims that it is love, or the striving after harmony, that makes the body a functioning whole as well as music a tempering influence upon the mind. Eryximachus is one of the early speakers in the dialogue, and his opinions, together with the other speakers', appear rather shallow in light of Socrates' famous speech near the end. Although we need not be overly subtle in reading the epigraph, it is important to realize that we are not reading a metaphysical dictum by Plato, but simply a bit of classical musical theory. The sentence means that the study of music is the study of how harmony and rhythm may be regulated so as to produce a tempering of the desires and a sympathy among men.

Crane is not suggesting that music is a way of approaching a real ideal of Love or that the Bridge, as a kind of visual music, is also a path to that ideal. It would be more correct to say, bearing in mind Crane's quite sophisticated understanding of Plato's methodology, that music is a way of stabilizing the emotions by giving them a protected setting, apart from actual situations in the

---

[17] Plato, *Laws,* trans. A. E. Taylor, in Hamilton and Cairns, p. 1225 ff.

Vision of the Voyage

world, in which they can be expressed. And this function of music is demonstrated by the Brooklyn Bridge in "Atlantis." In all the earlier sections of the poem, we have seen aspiration, love, disappointment, and destruction under the aspects of specific situations in life. Crane has considered how values shape experience and, these failing and the world crumbling, how new ones are born and a new world is created. He has explored how these values protect themselves by concealing the suffering which supports them. And he has discovered repeatedly the joy of threatening the reality of his own world in order to appreciate the abundant, endlessly fascinating manifestations of value in his own larger mind, his culture. That thrilling and terrifying adventure has composed the poems of *The Bridge*. Now in "Atlantis" Crane uses the Brooklyn Bridge, his central symbol, as a means of representing, without regard to specific circumstances, how his own mind operates or how consciousness itself operates.

The continuing interest of Romantics in generating a new style for apprehending reality may now be seen to have implied this goal, the representation of consciousness, all along. And their use of the "meaningful meaningless," which led in Crane's case to a use of metaphor sustaining a tension between the world and the categories of the understanding, makes it possible not only to create new meanings but at last to consider meaningfulness in its own right. This is finally the only stay against the despair resulting from the type of introspective analysis we have seen throughout *The Bridge*. The *eternal possibility* of value, or love, actually manifested only in situations of dissolution and hopelessness, presents to the individual a means of sustenance not dependent on specific value definitions.

Now we can see why a poem filled with clearly delineated people and problems should be concluded with a complex description of an object which, in a sense, has nothing to do with any of them. Notice how "Atlantis" begins. The sense of motion, grace, and power implied by the Bridge's structure commands our respect not for what it means, but simply because

The Bridge: *The Meaning of Suffering*

it must mean *something*. The first stanza introduces this respect and the second begins to identify it in the most general terms with human aspiration. Perhaps a paraphrase of the quotation ("Make thy love sure—to weave whose song we ply!") in this stanza would be helpful. All the ships which have ever sailed seem to be crying to the Bridge: do not fail us, for it is our mission to express your meaningfulness. The third stanza goes on to suggest that the imagination, represented by the moon and stars, construes the undefined meaningfulness of the Bridge into specific goals or directions. In the fourth stanza ("Sheerly the eyes, like seagulls stung with rime") Crane introduces the problem of the meaning of cultural values under the mysterious aspect of time. This is the point at which pessimism as a response to loss must be appreciated. And the world of specific values in time is the scene of all life, so Jason, representing man-at-sea, is now seen in stanza five ("Like hails, farewells—up planet-sequined heights") launching out into that hazardous world. All this goes through the poet's mind as he contemplates the structure of the Bridge, and it is summed up in the sixth stanza ("From gulfs unfolding, terrible of drums"). Interestingly the Bridge is conceived as transcending opposites, lifting night into day: that power is the heart of the Hegelian *aufheben*. The limitations of cultural values may be said to derive from the apprehension of reality in terms of opposites. When alternatives are mutually exclusive, action must reach an impasse. But the Bridge, "Vision-of-the-Voyage," represents the self-transcending character of thought, which is forever eluding opposites and reconstruing knower and known into novel problem situations. The power of love, as Crane suggests by seeing the Bridge as its "Paradigm," lies in the independence of that response, its resistance to characterization. The category "beloved" is infinite: we can love anything.

In the seventh stanza ("We left the haven hanging in the night") the poet is embarking, as it were, upon meaningful action, and the following stanzas suggest the paradoxes he encounters reflecting upon it. The main point made in stanza

Vision of the Voyage

eight ("O Thou steeled cognizance whose leap commits") about the symbolization of thought in the sweep of cables is a contrast with the bird's flight which we noted in "To Brooklyn Bridge." The curve of the winging sea gull or, here, of the lark is instantly lost in time. But the curves of the Bridge's cables repeat the same movement again and again. The Bridge suspends for the poet in one symbolic gesture the two notions which constitute "becoming." Birth and death, being and nonbeing lose their distinct opposition and their objectivity. Thus, Crane can say that conceiving experience on the model of the Bridge drains "death" of its awesome reality. And the actual agony of becoming, of living one's finite life in time, with which all the preceding lyrics were concerned, is now accepted joyfully. Crane is not merely forgetting the reality of loss: he is celebrating forgetfulness itself as the mind's greatest blessing. It is forgetfulness which makes the Deity's name and Pledge of stanza ten ("Forever Deity's glittering Pledge, O Thou") forever young.

Perhaps the subtlest point of "Atlantis" is contained in stanza eleven ("Migrations that must needs void memory"). Here it is clear that the Bridge and Love are not identified, for Crane says that a full knowledge of what the Bridge means would be unbearable to Love. Love cannot be made aware of the sacrifices required for its sake. Those "inventions that cobblestone the heart" could well refer to the war planes of "Cape Hatteras" or to any of the miseries which are actually born from our values. The poet sees the *price* of Love symbolized in the Bridge; therefore, he asks pardon for the way Love must manifest herself in the world. But like Emily Dickinson he appeals to an amoral judge, the Anemone. The last picture we have of the poet is his appeal to the silent beauty of this sea flower to sustain the brightness and clarity of his self-consciousness unjustified. Then Crane turns back to the Bridge for the final question and its answer of silence.

Epilogue:
Against Conclusions

It is possible to see in Crane's suicide the inevitable outcome of his life and work. But such a judgment appears sentimental after a study of *White Buildings* and *The Bridge*. After such a study Crane's suicide takes on an irresolvable ambiguity. For we have seen that no single part of any experience—in poetry or in life—is "true" enough to interpret all the rest of experience. This is especially important to understand when considering the centrality of pessimism to Romantic ways of thinking. To see through the "redeeming" aspects of life is not to vitiate meaningfulness itself. Therefore, *the* meaning of the Brooklyn Bridge in Crane's great poem always eludes us, just as *the* meaning of life can never be formulated. The implications of this strange truth are paradoxical. One of its most difficult implications is that Romantic suffering is not submission to the world. It is the mind challenging itself to comprehend experience more deeply: it is a highly demanding personal discipline. "Discipline" before the nineteenth century referred almost exclusively to the institutionalization of the personality. Discipline was what was required in order to reconcile oneself with being *somebody*. But in the nineteenth century a new kind of discipline appeared: the continuing effort of the mind to deprive itself of the security of

Vision of the Voyage

consistent institutionalized behavior, so that the price paid for one's validational categories could be seen. The theory of the penetration of masks which I have applied to Crane's poetry is intended to demonstrate that form of suffering and discipline in the twentieth century as well. But I should end by saying that in such a discipline there can be no conclusion.

Crane's last poem, "The Broken Tower," is concerned with this problem. The image of the title symbolizes the institution, whether of society or of the personality, in a state of crisis. The first four stanzas suggest that institutionalization results from the power of a symbol, the bells, to structure generalized appearances. But the poet must suffer a kind of exile since the meaning of the bells is not stable for him. He is as much the slave of symbolization as anyone else, but his own imagination structures the sounds into private meanings. The fifth stanza summarizes the whole program of introspective analysis we have followed in *The Bridge,* and the sixth brings us to the point of self-doubt Crane reached in "The Tunnel." The last four stanzas are for our purposes here the most important. For Crane suggests that his inability to know for sure whether any conceptualization of experience would ever be strong enough to defeat despair is due to the unpredictability of his own responses. As we saw beginning with Crane's "General Aims and Theories," his poetic method has always been to honor and record private experiences rather than to judge them by public standards. Does his latent power being stirred by someone's sweet mortality, his being healed at the end of the poem, amount to some reconciliation of conceptualization and experience?

The woman referred to in stanza seven is probably Peggy Cowley, who was, it is thought, the first woman Crane loved. And it is possible to read these last stanzas as a celebration of the sense of rightness and wholeness Crane may have felt as he was able to reconcile his personal sexual experience with one of the strongest "generalized appearances" of our society, heterosexual love. The fact is, of course, that Crane leaves this possibility

Epilogue: Against Conclusions

suspended. Rather than insisting upon his own independence in sustaining himself without "need" for another, he lets independence itself become problematical. Does "whose pulse" in stanza eight refer to "my blood" or "she" in the preceding stanza?

> The steep encroachments of my blood left me
> No answer (could blood hold such a lofty tower
> As flings the question true?)—or is it she
> Whose sweet mortality stirs latent power?—
>
> And through whose pulse I hear, counting the strokes
> My veins recall and add, revived and sure
> The angelus of wars my chest evokes:
> What I hold healed, original now, and pure . . .

The ambiguity is significant. For it suggests that Crane is able now to profit as much from considering the individual being of another as from considering his own. He has gone beyond the analyses of love we saw in "Voyages" and in various sections of *The Bridge*. Other people need not exist to the poet as generalized appearances, and they may be recognized without being used for victimizing interests. We may say that the whole discipline represented in *The Bridge* prepares the individual not only to destroy the sense of his own reality, but equally to honor reality in another person. In this way love stops being a form of personal management.

   Crane's conception of love takes into account both the natural perversity of experience and the radical individuality of people. This mode of apprehending another, as we saw in "Cape Hatteras" with regard to Whitman, was prepared for from the beginnings of Romanticism. The separation of self (uncharacterized being) from personality or role (characterized individuality for the purposes of problem solving) makes possible a kind of validation which does not rely upon the categories of "goodness" as opposed to "evil" in one's culture. The recognition of self, in the Romantic sense, is a description of incommensurable individuality. It is an honorific assertion, saying: I am important in spite of any characterization others would urge me to accept. (The notion that Romanticism asserts the "goodness" of man derives from a misconception of this sanctification of the self. It is beyond cultural definition and thus beyond good and evil.) Therefore, if the individual is smart enough and strong enough to penetrate the masks which stabilize his own egotism (the belief that his importance is greater than another's) then he can perhaps make an honorific assertion of (uncharacterized) value and being in another person. This is Crane's conception of love, I believe, in "The Broken Tower." The restored tower at the end of the poem does not represent a successful institutionalization of the personality, but a strength of soul which transcends the illusions of the "broken world" in order to make love possible. Is love a sentimentality? Let the reader bear the burden of his own conclusion.

Index

Alienation, 23, 26-27, 31, 36, 44, 58-61, 70-71, 73-74, 76-77, 104-105
Anaxagoras, 4
Anaximenes, 4
Aristotle, 7
Arnold, Matthew, 27; Switzerland series, 104
Blake, William, 160; "Morning," 161-162
Brooklyn Bridge, 112-115, 138, 141, 163, 166-174, 175
Carlyle, Thomas, 39; "Centre of Indifference," 61; *Sartor Resartus*, 29
Cézanne, Paul, 58
Chaplin, Charlie, 58-60, 86
Coleridge, Samuel Taylor, 24, 25-26, 33-35; "Eolian Harp," 29; "Kubla Khan," 78; "Nightmare Life-in-Death," 61; "Ode on the Departing Year," 28; "The Rime of the Ancient Mariner," 59
Columbus, 115-118, 120, 123, 126, 127, 135, 140, 145, 146, 165, 166, 168
Cowley, Peggy, 176
Crane, Hart: affinity with earlier Romantics, 31, 33-42, 49, 57, 60, 94; writings: "Atlantis," 149, 166-174; "At Melville's Tomb," 95-96, 139, 147; "Ave Maria," 115-118, 120, 140, 145; "Black Tambourine," 55-56; *The Bridge*, 33, 37, 42, 62, 96, 109-174, 176, 177; "The Broken Tower," 176-178, "To Brooklyn Bridge," 101, 112-115, 123, 147, 163, 174; "Cape Hatteras," 139-150, 174, 177; "Chaplinesque," 58-60, 65, 66, 83, 135; "Cutty Sark," 136-139, 168; "The Dance," 128-134, 136; "Emblems of Conduct," 63-65; "The Fernery," 55, 135; 'For the Marriage of Faustus and Helen," 50, 85-94, 104, 105, 112, 113, 120, 130, 146, 151, 155; "Garden Abstract," 50-51, 53; "General Aims and Theories," 37-38, 66, 176; "The Harbor Dawn," 118-121, 128, 129, 131, 137, 150; "Indiana," 134-136, 137, 144, 168; "Lachrymae Christi," 79-85, 129, 133, 147, 152; "Legend," 42-45, 51, 81, 88, 89, 133; letter to Gorham Munson, 17 March 1926, 34, 36, 170; "My Grandmother's Love Letters," 45-46, 51, 120-121; "National Winter Garden," 153-154, 157; "North Labrador," 54, 55, 61; "Paraphrase," 61-62, 65; "Passage," 75-79; "Pastorale," 52-53; "Praise for an Urn," 56-59; "Possessions," 65-68, 69, 78, 89, 102, 153; "Powhatan's Daughter," 120, 135; "Quaker Hill," 156-161, 164, 168; "Repose of Rivers," 62-63; "Recitative," 68-71, 90, 141; "The River," 123, 128, 129, 142, 147; "In Shadow," 52, 53-54, 55; "Southern

179

Index

Cross," 151-153, 155; "Stark Major," 51-52, 53; "Sunday Morning Apples," 47-50, 64, 162; "Three Songs," 150-155, 164; "The Tunnel," 156, 157, 160, 161-166, 168, 176; "Van Winkle," 120-123, 124, 128, 129; "Virginia," 154; "Voyages," 50, 96-106, 119, 141, 150, 177; *White Buildings*, 37, 42-107, 175; "The Wine Menagerie," 71-75, 131, 132, 137, 157
Crisis, 19, 26-27, 30, 31, 40, 47, 60-61, 157, 160, 176
Dérangement des sens, 47
Dickinson, Emily, 156-157, 161, 174
Ding an sich, 11, 23
Duncan, Isadora, 156-157, 161
Emerson, Ralph Waldo, 36
Empedocles, 4
Eliot, T.S., 31, 37, 106
Ginsberg, Allen, 140
Greenberg, Samuel, 63
Hegel, G. W. F., 1, 14-19, 15n, 17n, 38n, 54n, 168; "Absolute Knowledge," 38, 64, 106; *aufheben*, 113, 136, 173; cognition and objectivity, 16, 21, 42; epistemology, 14, 18, 29; "false infinite," 54; mediation, 16-17; negativity, 16-17, 18; "negation of the negation," 113, 135;*Phenomenology*, 2, 14-20, 30; versus Kant, 23; "Unhappy Consciousness," 111
Helen, 86-93, 120, 130, 134
Heraclitus, 4, 5, 6
Hume, David, 11
Imagination, 19, 25-26, 33-34, 57, 60, 96-106
Irony, 8, 13, 26, 31, 48, 58, 60, 77, 79
Job, 109-110, 135, 139, 149-150
Jonson, Ben: *The Alchemist*, 86, 94
Kahn, Otto, 38
Kant, Immanuel, 10-13, 14, 18-19, 22, 23; affinity with the Enlightenment, 13, 18; categorical imperative, 12-13; *Critique of Judgment*, 11; *Critique of Practical Reason*, 11; *Critique of Pure Reason*, 10, 11; epistemology, 10-11; ethics, 22
Kaufmann, Walter, 2n, 15n
Keats, John: "La Belle Dame sans Merci," 53, "negative capability," 73; "Ode on a Grecian Urn," 53; "Ode to a Nightingale," 28, 53, 125
Kierkegaard, Søren, 9n
Laforgue, Jules, 58, 86
Locke, John, 11
Mallarmé, Stéphane, 58
Maquokeeta, 129-134, 145-146, 168
Marlowe, Christopher, 86; *Hero and Leander*, 150; *Tamburlaine*, 117
Mask, 39-42, 43, 45, 48, 49, 58, 66, 71, 74, 76, 77, 88, 111, 134, 138
Mead, George Herbert, 21n
Meaningful meaningless, 43, 65
Mediation, 16-31, 38-42, 71. *See also* Hegel
Melville, Herman, 40, 94-96; "The Temeraire," 137, 139
Metaphor, 33, 43-44, 46-47, 63, 70, 72, 79, 81, 83, 85, 97-98, 131, 146, 160-161, 164
Metaphysics, 2-31; constitutive, 3-14, 15, 17, 18, 22, 26, 28, 29, 31, 35, 41, 64; hierarchic, 5, 30; self-transcending, 15-31
Nature, 22-23, 51
Nelson, Ernest, 56-58, 94, 166
Nietzsche, Friederich: "bad-conscience" 27; *The Birth of Tragedy*, 84-86; "will to truth," 64, "will to power," 75
Organicism, 19-20
Parmenides, 6
Peckham, Morse, 26n, 27n
Pierrot, 57, 86
Plato, 59, 11, 35, 85, 110, 137, 156; *Apology*, 8n; *Dialogues*, 18; epistemology, 6-7; ethics, 7; *Laws*, 171; metaphysics, 7; *Republic*, 7; *Symposium*, 7n, 170-171
Pocahontas, 120, 123, 124-125, 128, 129-132, 134, 142
Poe, Edgar Allan, 164-165; "The City in the Sea," 165; "The Raven," 165
Pre-Socratics, 4-5
Protagoras, 6
Pythagorus, 4
Redemption, 28-29, 36, 40, 54, 58, 60, 73, 76, 81, 111, 114
Rimbaud, Arthur, 42
Rip Van Winkle, 121-122, 123
Ruskin, John, 29

Index

Sartre, Jean Paul, 74; *No Exit*, 54
Satan, 109
Sehnsucht, 23, 25
Self-as-other, 21
Seneca: *Medea*, 115, 140
Socrates, 8
Sommer, William 49, 64
Sophists, 5-8, 9, 11
Stevens, Wallace, 43
Stimulus and response, 20-22, 35, 66
Tate, Allen, 107, 167
Tennyson, Alfred, Lord: "The Lady of Shallot," 53,
Thales, 4, 5
Transcendentalism, 36, 58, 73, 76
Turbayne, Colin Murray, 47n

Wagner, Richard, 98
Winters, Yvor, 38
Whitman, Walt, 36, 94, 124, 139-150, 158, 162, 177; Calamus poems, 144, 156; "Out of the Cradle Endlessly Rocking," 144; "Passage to India," 139-141, 146; "Song of Myself," 148; "Years of the Modern," 148
Wordsworth, William, 23, 76, 87; "Elegiac Stanzas," 29; "Intimations Ode," 28; "Lines Composed above Tintern Abbey," 28, 62; Lucy poems, 104; "Resolution and Independence," 136; *Prelude*, 62, 77
Yeats, William Butler: "The Cat and the Moon," 57

181

WITHDRAWN